Inside the Dzanga-Sangha Rain Forest

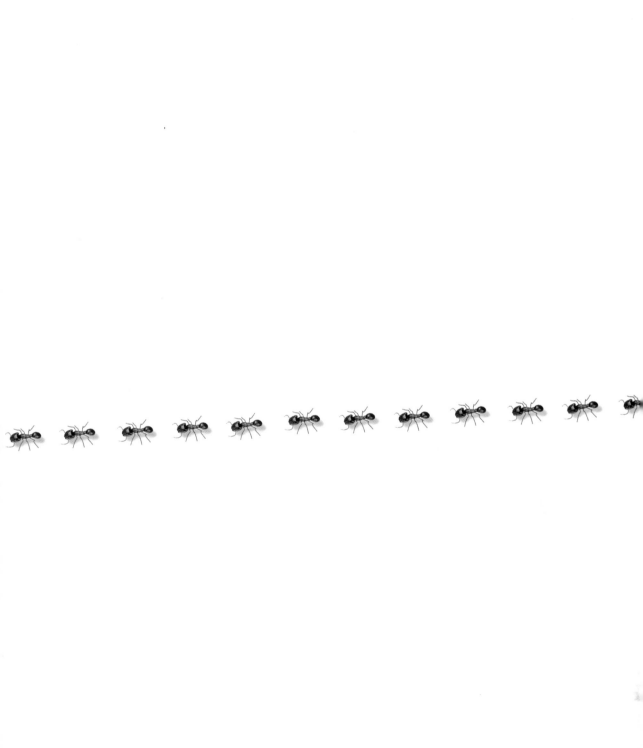

Inside the Dzanga-Sangha Rain Forest

From the working journals of the
scientists, artists, and filmmakers
on expedition for the
American Museum of Natural History

Compiled by Francesca Lyman

WORKMAN PUBLISHING • NEW YORK

Library of Congress Cataloging-in-Publication
Inside the Dzanga-Sangha Rain Forest / compiled by Francesca Lyman
p.   cm.
Summary: An account of the American Museum of Natural History
expedition to the Dzanga-Sangha Rain Forest in the Central African
Republic to collect specimens for an exhibit.
ISBN 0-7611-0870-X
1. Natural history—Central African Republic—Dzanga-Sangha Rain
Forest—Juvenile literature. 2. Biological specimens—Central African
Republic—Dzanga-Sangha Rain Forest—Collection and preservation—
Juvenile literature. 3. Dzanga-Sangha Rain Forest history (Central
African Republic)—Juvenile literature. [1. Natural history—Central
African Republic. 2. Biological specimens—Central African Republic—
Collection and preservation. 3. Dzanga-Sangha Rain Forest (Central
African Republic)] I. Lyman, Francesca. II. American Museum of
Natural History.
QH195.C38I57 1998
508.6741—dc21

Designed by Barbara Balch

Published by
Workman Publishing Company, Inc.
708 Broadway
New York, NY 10003–9555

Manufactured in Italy
First printing July 1998
10 9 8 7 6 5 4 3 2 1

Contents

Preface 7

About the Authors 8

1
Getting Ready 11

2
Getting There 21

3
Welcome to Dzanga-Sangha 31

4
A Village of Elephants 47

5
Getting to Work 61

6
People of the Rain Forest 73

7
Deep Forest Site 83

8
The Great Apes 93

9
Life at the Lodge 103

10
Last Days 119

11
Building the Exhibit 125

With thanks to Joyce A. Cloughly, Naomi A.
Echental, Denis Finnin, Phillip L. Fraley, Barrett
A. Klein, Alec Madoff, Michael A. Rapkiewicz,
Maron L. Waxman, and Rena Zurofsky of the
American Museum of Natural History. Thanks
also go to Barbara Balch, Giema Tsakuginow,
and most especially to Michaela Muntean
of Workman Publishing Company.

There was never any question; it had to be a rain forest. Although tropical rain forests cover only 7 percent of the earth's land surface, they are home to half of the known plant and animal species in the world. As the centerpiece of the American Museum of Natural History's new Hall of Biodiversity, no environment could better illustrate the rich variety and interdependence of plant and animal life.

Museum scientists and designers envisioned an exhibit that would show the wonders of a rain forest along with the ever-growing threats to its existence. By re-creating a lifelike, life-size section of forest, the Museum would give visitors a sense of what it was like to walk beneath the towering, vine-tangled trees. They would hear the calls of birds and chattering of monkeys. And, thanks to a continuously running film, they'd be able to see many rain forest animals as they moved and traveled through the forest.

It would take hundreds of people over 2 years to plan and design the exhibit.

It would take 20 scientists, artists, and filmmakers 6 weeks in a tropical rain forest to research and collect the necessary materials.

It would take another 18 months to build and mount the exhibit.

This is the story of how many people, working together, created a rain forest inside a museum.

Geralyn Abinader, a member of the American Museum of Natural History exhibition staff, has worked with the audiovisual department on numerous projects including a video about African elephants. In the Central African Republic, she directed the videos that are installed in the rain forest exhibit. *"The greatest thing about this trip was that I had no idea*

what to expect. I had no frame of reference because I'd never been to Africa. I couldn't even picture myself there. It was a total unknown—so new, so exciting!"

During her childhood in Africa, **Pamela Beresford** became interested in African birds and mammals. Now a graduate student in the Department of Ornithology at the Museum, she is working toward her Ph.D. in ecology and evolutionary biology. In the Dzanga-Sangha rain forest, Ms. Beresford studied the diversity of African forest birds. *"I've always had an interest in ornithology— the study of birds—and was particularly drawn to African grey parrots. In the Dzanga-Sangha rain forest I got a rare opportunity to study these fascinating birds in the wild. I also enjoyed sharing some of the things I know about birds with the kids who helped us at the deep forest site."*

Joel Cracraft, Ph.D., Curator of Ornithology at the Museum, was the chief scientist in Dzanga-Sangha. He was the primary director of the installation of the rain forest exhibit. Dr. Cracraft also teaches at Columbia University and has an appointment at City University of New York. *"All rain forests are different, but the Dzanga-Sangha rain forest, with its spectacular diversity, is special. You never know what surprise awaits you—a sudden encounter with an elephant or gorilla, or a quiet, enchanting moment with butterflies or birds. We have tried to put both experiences in the Museum's rain forest diorama."*

For the past 8 years, **Brian Morrissey** has worked as an artist, designer, and exhibit preparator at the Museum, helping to create many exhibits as well as the new Hall of Human Biology and Evolution. In Dzanga-Sangha, he collected and photographed plants and insects, translated a lot of French into English, and made a long 3-pointer in the basketball game. *"One of the great pleasures was getting to know some of the local people—a good reminder that people are basically the same everywhere. In spite of the vastly different cultures and lifestyles, our similarities were far greater than our differences."*

Stephen C. Quinn is Senior Production Manager in the Department of Exhibitions and Graphics at the Museum, overseeing the creation of many exhibits. He supervised the collection of plant and animal specimens in Dzanga-Sangha, collecting many himself. *"My parents took me to the American Museum of Natural History for the first time when I was 4 years old. According to them, I announced that 'Someday I'd like to work here.' It's hard to believe I knew at such an early age what I wanted to do. Traveling to Africa as part of the collecting team was a dream come true, and working in the rain forest is an experience I shall never forget."*

Team leader and photographer in Dzanga-Sangha, **Willard Whitson** has been designing and developing exhibitions for natural history and science museums for 20 years. He is currently the Associate Director of Exhibits at the American Museum of Natural History. *"I had been to Africa many times before, but each trip is a new experience in this land of amazingly diverse landscapes and cultures. There are the sweeping savannas of Kenya, the ruggedly beautiful coast of South Africa and, of course, the lush, tropical density of the forests of the Central African Republic."*

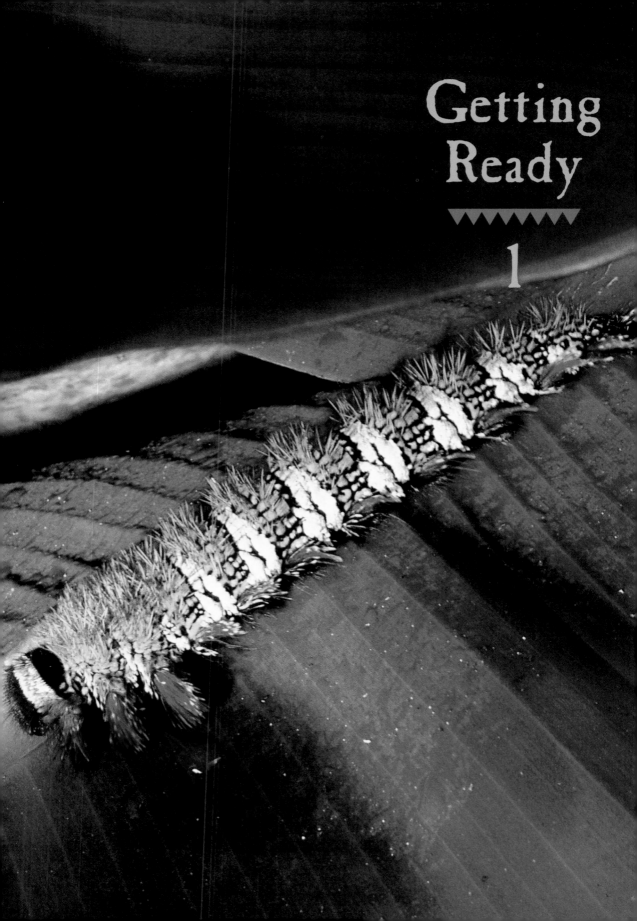

Getting
Ready

1

> **"We could use some good advice. Most of the crew have never been to Africa, let alone a Congo rain forest."**

Long before we left for the Dzanga-Sangha rain forest in Africa, designers and scientists began working on plans for the exhibit. An enormous amount of information and equipment would be needed to re-create the look and feel of the Dzanga-Sangha rain forest. To collect everything while we were there, we would need over 6,000 pounds of supplies including, among many other things, gallons of plaster to make impressions of leaves; rubber to make molds of tree bark; supplies for sketching and painting, writing and photographing; video cameras, film, tape recorders, cable cord, and walkie-talkies; gloves, dust masks, propane torches, rubber bands, bottles, pliers, scissors, and saws. There would be hundreds of kinds of bags, boxes, and containers needed to store and transport vines, leaves, and samples of rocks and soil. All these things plus tents, mosquito netting, tool kits, and medical supplies had to be sent to Dzanga-Sangha so they would be there when we arrived.

> "We had considered journeying to the rain forests of South America or southeast Asia, but both have been widely written about and explored. Far less is known about African rain forests."

What to Pack

- Neutral-colored, lightweight clothing because of the heat

- Socks and closed shoes to stop chigger fleas and other insects that attack the feet

- No deep or bright blue clothing, as it attracts tsetse flies

WARNING: Make sure your clothing dries after washing it. Certain types of flies lay eggs in damp fabric and can even bore into your skin. If they do, you can kill them by covering the spot with Vaseline (this suffocates them).

AREAS OF RAIN FOREST AROUND THE WORLD

At one time, rain forests stretched in an almost continuous belt around the earth, broken only by bodies of water. It is estimated that half of the world's tropical rain forests have already been lost, largely due to human activities. Today, small areas of rain forest can be found in southeast Asia, Malaysia, the Philippines, and Australia. The largest rain forest is the Amazon, in South America. The second largest—about 20 percent of the world's remaining rain forest—is in Africa.

Shown here is an aerial view of a section of the Dzanga-Sangha rain forest.

A group of 20 of us was selected to go on the expedition. We were chosen because of our special knowledge or skills. Some of us were artists who would draw and paint the plants and animals. Some were scientists such as ornithologists, who study birds, and mammalogists, who study mammals. The audiovisual crew would be responsible for recording the sights and sounds of the forest in order to create the background images that would be used in the exhibit. Those of us on the plant-collecting team would gather the plants that were needed. They had to be carefully selected and removed so as not to do any harm to the forest. We would select only plants

Pads

Tropical rain forests are ideal homes for amphibians, such as salamanders, toads, and frogs. Because they are cold-blooded, they do not generate their own body heat; instead, they soak up heat from the sun and air. Tree frogs are common in the rain forest. They have developed small suction pads on their toes, allowing them to climb and cling to leaves and branches.

"Sango is the national language of the Central African Republic. I wrote some common words and phrases out phonetically, so I'd be able to remember how to pronounce them."

bai saline, clearing

m-BEE-bar-ah-moh Good morning, Good evening

TOHN-gah-NAH-nee-aye? How are you?

Yah-pay I'm fine

seen-GAY-lay-MEEN-gee Thank you

bee-GUAY-ah-way Good-bye

BIG-EYED TREE FROG

that were found in large quantities and would grow back quickly. We would not, of course, take anything that was endangered. One of the main reasons for the exhibit, after all, was to show the many threats to the rain forest. All of us would help in preparing, preserving, and packing the plants to be sent to the Museum. It was estimated that we'd return with over 10,000 pounds of rain forest material.

Making Plans

At this point, our expedition leaders had the most work to do. With the help of the World Wildlife Fund, they made arrangements for trucks to transport our equipment and for jeeps to transport us. They made sure that the newly built lodge had enough room to house and feed all of us and that we'd have guides to help us in the rain forest. After many months of sending e-mail back and forth between New York and Africa, the arrangements were made.

All the while, we prepared ourselves for the jobs we would be doing in Dzanga-Sangha, researching and educating ourselves about the plants and animals. The official language of the Central African Republic is French, so some of us took French lessons or brushed up on the French we already knew. The national language, however, is Sango, and we memorized some phrases so we'd at least be able to say "Thank you" and "Good morning."

Everyone, of course, needed a passport and a visa. We also needed medical checkups and vaccination shots for yellow fever, malaria, typhoid, tetanus, polio, meningitis, and rabies. It seemed as if we were spending a lot of time in a doctor's office!

The excitement about going on the expedition wasn't perfect—we were going to be away from our

Energizers

Plants make other life on earth possible. Through a process known as photosynthesis, plants collect energy from sunlight and use this energy to turn water and carbon dioxide into a simple sugar called glucose. Glucose is what plants need to fuel their cells and make other substances that are necessary for their survival. In the process, the plants give off oxygen, and oxygen is what we and every other animal on earth need to survive.

CRAB SPIDER, CAMEROON

The Dzanga-Sangha rain forest is a small part of the larger section of rain forest that stretches from Uganda west to Cameroon, and from parts of the Democratic Republic of the Congo north to the Central African Republic. This area is known as the Congolese rain forest, or the Congo River Basin rain forest. The Congo River, at 2,900 miles, is the second-longest river in Africa. A vast, fan-shaped network of smaller rivers and streams flows downward into a central depression of land known as the Congo Basin, an area that covers nearly 1 1/2 million square miles.

Within the Congo rain forest are millions of species of plants and animals. Most—perhaps as much as 90 percent—have not yet been discovered by scientists.

A typical temperate forest in the United States might have, at most, 12 different kinds of trees. A tropical rain forest may have hundreds of different species. It has been estimated that a 4-mile square of

OLIVE BABOON, CENTRAL AFRICAN REPUBLIC

JOHNSTON'S CHAMELEON, DEMOCRATIC REPUBLIC OF THE CONGO

SCARAB BEETLE, CAMEROON

rain forest may contain as many as 1,500 species of flowering plants, 750 species of trees, 400 species of birds, 150 species of butterflies, 100 species of reptiles, and 60 species of amphibians. Because the tropics are warm year-round and get plenty of rain, a wide range of species can thrive. There may also be so many different species because rain forests have existed for many millions of years, and the plants and animals have had a long time to evolve and adapt.

FLOWER, CENTRAL AFRICAN REPUBLIC

Those adaptations have taken an immense variety of forms. Some plants and animals have adapted so specifically that they occur in a small, special area and nowhere else.

JEWELED TREE FROG, CAMEROON

MICRO MOTH, CONGO

Brilliantly colored flowers, such as this Flame of the Forest, attract birds and insects.

families for 6 weeks. There were no phones in the rain forest, of course, and there were few mail deliveries, so we probably wouldn't have any contact with wives, husbands, or children for the whole time we were there.

What Is a Tropical Rain Forest?

Tropical rain forests lie in a belt around the earth, straddling the invisible line known as the equator. This belt is called the tropics, and it stretches from the Tropic of Cancer to the Tropic of Capricorn. Unlike other parts of the world, the tropics are always about the same distance from the sun. As a result, the sun rises and sets at about the same time every day, and the temperature is fairly consistent throughout the year. On average, rain forests receive about 80 inches of rain a year. Year-round sunlight, warmth, and wetness are ideal

Meet a Beetle

The hard-bodied darkling beetle is a scavenger that feeds on decaying vegetation, animal dung, and seeds.

DARKLING
BEETLE

conditions for encouraging life, and this is why rain forests have such a rich and varied range of plants and animals.

There is much about the way in which a rain forest works that we are just beginning to understand. One of the things we do know is that tropical rain forests play a crucial role in the world's weather patterns and climate. At the equator, the sun's rays hit the earth directly and their energy is concentrated in the tropics. Rain forest plants take in huge amounts of carbon dioxide and produce lots of oxygen. And oxygen, of course, makes all other life on earth possible. Rain forest plants also absorb an enormous amount of water. When the water evaporates, clouds form and it rains again. Both these processes play important parts in global weather cycles.

> "I've been working out at the gym and expect my arms to be stronger so that I'll be able to hold the camera for longer periods of time. I can't wait to get started."

Since 1945, more than half of the world's rain forests have been destroyed. The main reasons are that people use the trees for timber and the land for farms and grazing. Land is also cleared to mine for minerals, such as tin or diamonds. All of these uses add to forest destruction, of course, but an even greater threat is the building of roads, which in turn leads to more hunting of animals, land clearing, building, and farming.

When trees are cut down and burned, tons of carbon dioxide is released into the atmosphere, and all this carbon dioxide may be changing the earth's climate. Warmer global temperatures, rising sea levels, and the extinction of species that cannot adapt to the new conditions may be just some of

BaAka

"Pygmy" comes from a Greek word meaning "half an arm's length" or "the distance from knuckle to elbow." Because of their short stature, groups such as the BaAka are frequently referred to as pygmies. They dislike the name, though, and prefer to be known by their group, or tribal names. Most adults stand between 4½ and 5 feet tall.

Makiso, one of our BaAka guides, and Steve Quinn.

the prices we have to pay for destruction of tropical rain forests.

Why the Dzanga-Sangha Rain Forest?

Besides having rich and spectacular varieties of animal and plant life, Dzanga-Sangha is also home to the BaAka and many other ethnic groups. These peoples' lives and lifestyles have been intertwined with this rain forest for hundreds of years.

Remote and isolated, Dzanga-Sangha is difficult to get to. Yet it, too, was being threatened by logging and mining. For years, hunting was unlimited and greatly reduced the number of animals.

Much of that changed in 1986, when the government of the Central African Republic, along with a conservation group known as the World Wildlife Fund, established an area known as the Dzanga-Sangha Reserve. In some areas, hunting and mining were banned, and rangers were hired to patrol the parks and enforce the laws. Efforts were made to protect the rich and varied wildlife and at the same time to help the local people find new ways to support themselves and their families without destroying their environment.

> "Half of all the elephants in Africa live in Dzanga-Sangha, and the area itself is half-named for them—'Dzanga' means 'village of elephants.' "

The future of Dzanga-Sangha, like the future of rain forest areas around the world, depends on people understanding, appreciating, and learning to conserve their natural wealth and wonder. We set out on our expedition to help do all those things.

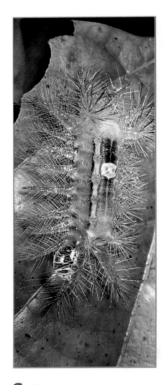

Spiney Caterpillar
The spines on this caterpillar blur its outline against the leaf on which it feeds, helping it to hide from predators.

Getting There

2

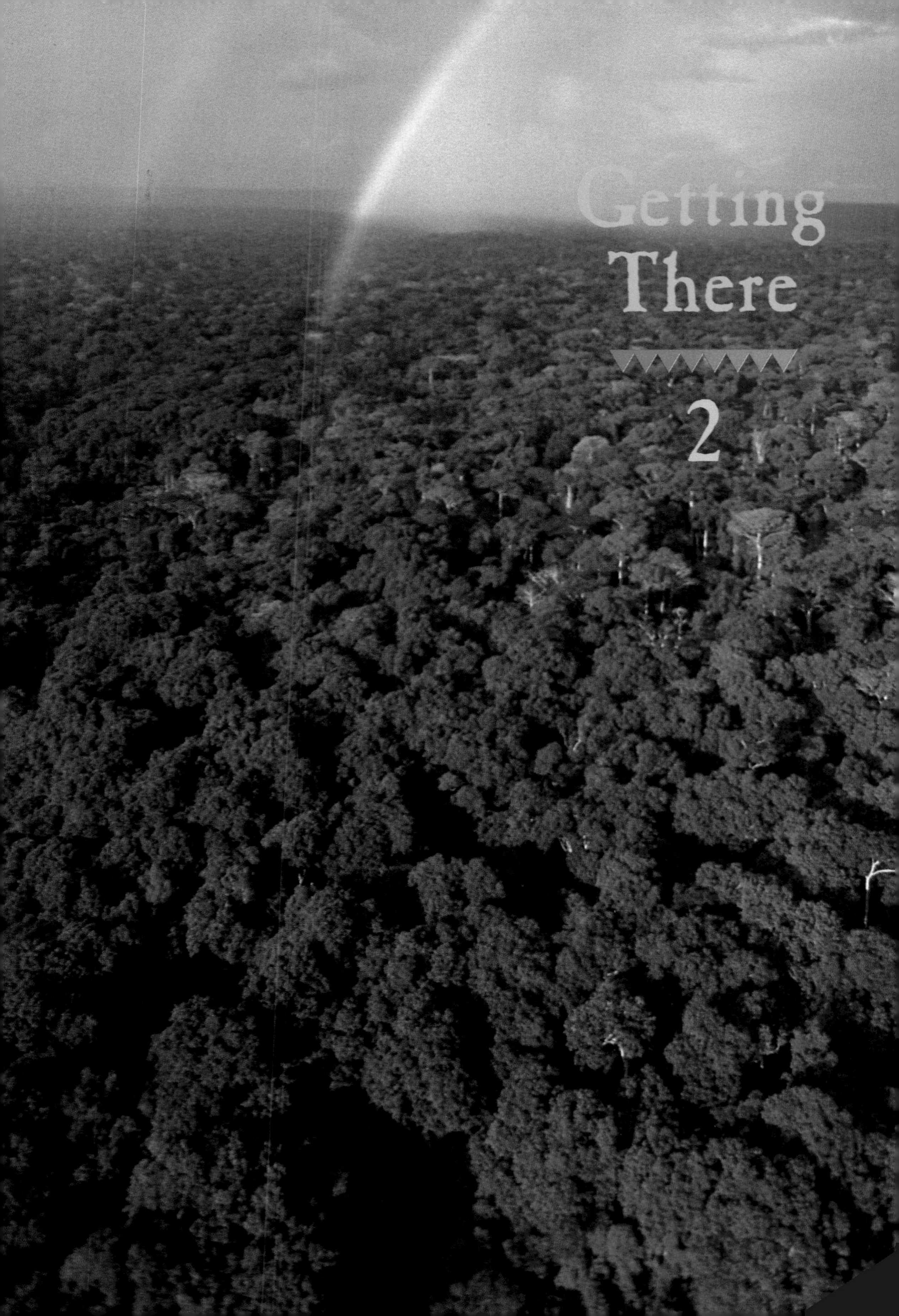

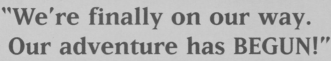

"We're finally on our way. Our adventure has BEGUN!"

To get to the **Dzanga-Sangha** rain forest, we crossed three continents, an ocean, a sea, and the largest desert in the world.

We set off from New York City and flew to Paris, France. From there we flew to Bangui, the capital city of the Central African Republic. To reach Bangui, we had to fly for 5 hours over the Sahara. From the air, it looked like a vast ocean of sand, with frozen "waves" that seemed to disappear into the horizon. The Sahara, which separates northern Africa from the rest of the continent, is so large that the entire continental United States could fit within its 3 million square miles.

We arrived in Bangui at night, exhausted after traveling for 31 hours. We would have one night in the city before heading to Bayanga, a small

Very Big Bugs

Goliath beetles are the giants of the insect world. Measuring 4 inches long, these beetles have wings that are bigger than those of a sparrow.

GOLIATH BEETLES, SHOWN HERE AT HALF THEIR ACTUAL SIZE

village on the edge of the rain forest. As we climbed off the plane, we were met at the airport by officials from the United States Embassy and guides who took us to our hotel.

The roads on the way to the hotel were lined with wood huts and corrugated tin houses. We saw people everywhere cooking food over open fires. Along the sides of the roads were stalls and market areas which were closed for the night.

> "The air was cloudy with smoke and cinders from the cooking fires. People stood by the side of the road cooking, mingling, and selling things."

There were many women about—some wearing wonderfully colorful clothing. Most were carrying bundles of firewood on their heads. It was the way almost all the local people carried just about everything.

Right: Style and dress in Africa are as diverse as its people and its lands.

CENTRAL AFRICAN REPUBLIC

The Central African Republic, or C.A.R., a country almost exactly in the middle of Africa, has a population of about 3,000,000. From 1887 until it received complete independence in 1960, this part of Africa was a colony of France. Bangui, the capital city of the Central African Republic, is on the northern bank of the Ubangi River, across from the Democratic Republic of the Congo. More than 1,000,000 people live in Bangui.

Scientists have been able to identify about 850,000 species of insects. But there are likely 30 million—or more—species that have not yet been "discovered." The study of insects—their enormous variety and fascinating behavior—is a field of science called entomology. Shown here is a mantid.

Bangui was lively at night. We passed a three-sided building where music was playing and people were dancing. Along the side of the road, children were catching grasshoppers. They would then roast them on a stick or string and sell them to motorists as snacks. Local men carried trays on their head, laden with what looked like caramel-covered popcorn balls.

"Just outside Bangui, many houses were made of wood or mud-brick and had tin roofs. Farther out, the houses were made of wattle and mud with thatched roofs in a peaked design. Then we saw circular mud huts with thatched roofs. Finally, there were simple domed huts made of branches and leaves."

The air was heavy with smoke from the countless cooking fires burning throughout the city. About halfway to the hotel, however, we noticed more smoke coming from inside our car than from outside. An alarming glow appeared under the dashboard. We were on fire! Our driver stopped the car and beat out the flames with his hands. He crammed all of us and our luggage into another vehicle, and we kept on driving to our hotel. We were glad to get there.

Capital Welcome

The next day in Bangui, we met with the country's top government officials. There were stories about our expedition in the Bangui newspapers and even on television and radio. Our expedition was important not just for the American Museum of Natural History, we discovered, but also

Inching Along

Inchworms, or measuring worms, are the larvae of certain types of moths. Because they do not have a middle pair of legs, they move by "inching" along—stretching the front part of their body and bringing the rear up to meet it.

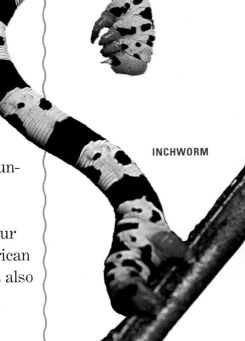

INCHWORM

BONGO

Bongos are large, colorful antelopes. Their coats are reddish brown with white stripes. They have black-and-white legs, and a head streaked with black markings. Both males and females have heavy spiral horns. Bongos live in small groups or pairs.

Duikers are small antelopes that grow no taller than 18 inches at the shoulder—about

BLUE DUIKER

the same height as a medium-sized dog. They have short legs, arched backs, and pointed hooves. They may have short, straight, or slightly curved horns. Duikers usually travel alone or in pairs.

Sitatungas are difficult to spot in the forest. These antelopes spend most of the daylight hours near swampy areas hiding, resting, or standing in the water. At night they come ashore to feed on forest undergrowth and leaves of bushes. Only adult male sitatungas have horns.

A FEMALE SITATUNGA AND CALF

for the Central African Republic. Our Museum exhibit would bring attention and, the government hoped, more visitors to the area.

The next morning, our crew divided into two groups: one group would fly to Bayanga in a small, nine-seater plane. The other group would be driven there by one of the guides, taking some of the equipment and supplies with them.

Those who went by plane took off into a hazy, overcast sky. Still, they could see the rain forest spread out below like a vast green carpet broken only by the snaky lines of rivers, which cut through the green like long scars. A little over an hour later, the plane set down at the Bayanga "airport"—a dirt landing strip.

"The people were friendly and said 'hello,' although we did get suspicious glances from some. The little kids sometimes stared at us and then giggled uncontrollably when we walked up to them and shook their hands. They had seen white people before, of course, but it was still a fairly rare occurrence."

Those who traveled the old-fashioned way—by jeep—climbed into an incredibly beat-up 4×4 and headed west. It was 350 miles from Bangui to Bayanga, but only the first 20 miles of the road were paved. Trucks filled with wood passed us on their way back to Bangui. There were also people pushing and pulling carts filled with logs, sticks, and branches. Some people walked with stacks of wood piled on their head. All the wood was being brought in from the forest to fuel the nightly cooking fires.

When the paved road ended, we were on a one-lane dirt road not much wider than a hiking trail.

Sunbird

The lower neck and chest of the scarlet-crested sunbird is, as its name suggests, a bright crimson red. These birds are quite common in Dzanga-Sangha, and a pair will often nest year after year in the same tree.

Orb weaver spiders have 8 eyes arranged in 2 rows with 4 eyes in each row. Many orb weavers spin an entire new web every day.

It was like driving through a tunnel—a dark green tunnel with thickly tangled growth on either side and vine-draped trees overhead. We'd been told the road wasn't good, but we never imagined how terrible it actually was. Pitted with potholes 2 feet deep and rutted with sand, the road was treacherously bumpy. It didn't help that our driver, Patrice, insisted on driving 50 miles an hour. We bumped and raced along, stirring up huge clouds of red dust from the unpaved road. It was too hot to close the windows, so the dust poured in and covered everything, including us. We spent most of the trip with bandannas wrapped around our faces and our sunglasses on, even after it became pitch-dark.

Every 30 or 40 miles we passed a village of several hundred people. Some villages had small plots cleared for gardens; some had a few animals, such as chickens and goats. As we raced by, the

FLOWER FLY, CAMEROON

Right: Looping, climbing, clinging, twisting, and floating—rain forest plants have developed a vast number of ways of growing in order to get as much sunlight as possible.

people—especially the kids—would point at us and wave.

Occasionally an oncoming car would appear. The drivers would race toward each other until the last possible second, then they'd swerve into the bush, crashing into tree branches. In the 13 hours it took us to get to Bayanga, we had three near-crashes. We arrived covered in red dust from head to toe. On the trip, we did catch sight of some brightly colored sunbirds and forest antelopes—large, majestic bongos and small, dainty duikers.

Hello, Doli!

We arrived late that night at Doli Lodge, our home for the next 6 weeks. The lodge had been built recently and was much nicer than we had expected. There were four bungalows on stilts, all built from native redwood. Each bungalow had two apartments, and each apartment had a bedroom with two beds in it, a bathroom, and a porch that overlooked the Sangha River. The bathrooms had hand-held showers, but with cold water only.

Unfortunately, the bathrooms also came equipped with waterbugs, gigantic spiders, and cockroaches at least 2 inches long. They seemed to pop up everywhere and cling to everything. It was our introduction to many weeks of living with insects of all kinds. Right now, though, we didn't care. We had been traveling for 4 days. We were exhausted, but we were finally here—in the heart of the rain forest.

A Rat as Long as a Cat

The African giant pouched rat, also called the Gambian pouched rat, is a friendly rodent—if you don't mind its size. Some people even keep it as a pet. Its body measures 10 to 17 inches long, and its tail is about the same length. The giant pouched rat weighs between 2 and 6 pounds. Its name derives from the fact it has cheek pouches in which it carries food. Giant pouched rats feed on an assortment of vegetation as well as small insects and other invertebrates.

COCKROACH, ACTUAL SIZE

Welcome
to
Dzanga-
Sangha

3

> "It's so beautiful, I don't have words to describe it. It's not like our hemisphere at all."

When most people think of a tropical rain forest, they imagine a steamy, hot jungle. They may picture explorers hacking their way through thick undergrowth or Tarzan swinging on a vine between the trees. But that's a movie-style rain forest. In reality, a mature, uncut rain forest is quite easy to walk through. That's because the branches of the towering trees block the sunlight, so few plants grow on the forest floor.

All rain forest plants compete with one another for light. That competition helps give a rain forest its shape. Rain forest plants grow in layers, or bands, depending on how much light they receive.

Watch Your Step!

The Gabon viper usually reaches a length of about 4 feet, but some grow as long as 6 feet. Its complex, colorful markings serve as camouflage in the dappled sunlight of the forest. Gabon vipers feed on rodents and occasionally on birds and even monkeys.

GABON VIPER

Right: A colorful mosaic of decaying leaves and flowers on the forest floor.

Broad-leaved plants and ferns are among the few types of vegetation that are able to grow in the dim light of the forest floor.

Each layer gets less light than the layer above it. The strongest, hottest sunlight on earth beats down on the top of a tropical rain forest, but only a tiny fraction—perhaps as little as 1 percent—reaches the forest floor.

Starting at the Bottom

Nearly all life in the rain forest begins, ends, and begins again on the shadowy forest floor. The floor is carpeted with a shallow layer of leaf litter; the few plants that grow there, such as ferns and broad-leaved plants, have large, thin leaves that can absorb whatever

Battling Beetles

Rhinoceros beetles can grow up to 3 inches or more in length. Only the males have a pair of large horns on their head. The horns are used as weapons to battle rival males over food, females, or territory.

RHINOCEROS BEETLE

sunlight reaches them. We saw ginger plants whose large, succulent flowers seemed to grow right out of the ground. There were a number of ferns, their tongue-like leaves sliced with tiny slashes on either side.

The air was rich with strong smells—the odor of rotting wood, the fragrance of flowers growing on the forest floor or hanging from the trees.

Rain forest soil is some of the oldest on earth and, because of that, it is often poor in nutrients.

"We had spent months preparing for the jobs we would be doing here. But nothing could have pre-pared us for the richness and beauty of the rain forest."

Over many millions of years, rain has washed away minerals, leaving the soil less fertile. Nutrients in the rain forest are mostly found on top of the ground. As dead plants and animals fall to the forest floor, they quickly decompose in the heat and humidity. Many kinds of insects help speed up the process, breaking down the organic matter; after this the nutrients are immediately soaked up by the roots of nearby trees.

Magnificent trees, some as tall as 20-story buildings, make a start in the spongy layer of leaf litter and thin soil. Because the soil is so poor in nutrients, trees don't send roots deep into the ground. Many roots stay in the shallow layer of topsoil or break through the earth and grow along the ground. Because these shallow root systems do not give a tree much support, some trees have developed buttresses. These large growths spread out from the base of the tree like the folds of a gigantic swirling skirt.

Hairy What?

Clambering over other plants is the hairy cucumber vine, whose fruit bears a gaily striped, bright orange fuzz.

**FLUSHING
LEAVES**

Branches are useful to trees only in places where the leaves are exposed to light. For that reason, the lower trunks of most rain forest trees usually have no branches—the first branches frequently don't appear until 50 feet up from the base of the trunk.

Many trees and plants within the rain forest produce new leaves very quickly in a process called "flushing." The new leaves are often of such brilliant colors— reds, yellows, or light greens—that from a distance they look like flowers. In a few days, they gradually change their color to the dark green of mature leaves.

BUTTRESS ROOTS

Some rain forest trees develop roots in the form of large triangle-shaped buttresses to help support the weight of the tree.

STILT ROOTS

Smaller trees sometimes form stilt roots that offer increased support in the wet environment of the forest.

Trees are the framework of the forest. Without them, the rest of the rain forest community could not survive.

The Story of the Understory

The understory of the forest extends from the ground up to about 40 or 50 feet. It is home to shrubs and small trees that have adapted to getting hardly any light at all. The seedlings of larger trees are also there, waiting for a break in the forest layer above so that they can grow toward the light.

In the understory, nearly one in every four plants is a vine. Vines are climbing plants that try to hitch a ride up toward the light. Because vines don't have a woody trunk to support themselves, they have developed many strategies to get to the sunlight of the canopy above. Using barbed thorns, clasping roots, or curling tendrils,

"Even at high noon, it was dark inside the forest. Very little sunlight made its way through the thick canopy, so it was almost impossible for us to take photographs without using a flash."

they hook into, grab onto, or wind themselves around tree trunks and branches.

Lianas are woody vines that stretch up from the understory to the next layer of growth, then dangle down. Once they've reached the light of the canopy, lianas may spread out to other trees,

Rubiaceae, a shrub with small, heart-shaped leaves and bright red fruit, grows on the forest floor.

Let a Tree Be Your Umbrella

Umbrella trees, with their distinctive leaves, are among the most common in the forest. Found primarily along roads and at the edges of the forest, these fast-growing trees take advantage of areas where there is plenty of sunlight.

De Brazza's monkey is a guenon that stays in the lower regions of the forest. Adults measure 16 to 24 inches, with a tail as long as or longer than their body. Like most guenons, they have colorful, patterned faces. If a male senses danger, he will bark and shake branches to draw attention away from his group. De Brazza's monkeys eat fruit and seeds, and have been known to dig in leaf litter and mud on the forest floor, hunting for insects.

which can cause problems for the trees. If one tree falls, it can take others down with it, so some trees have developed a defense: they shed branches that have been entangled with a vine.

The Canopy—
The Leafy Roof of the Forest

More than 60 feet above the ground are the crowns of the medium-size trees. The trunks of these trees are usually fairly straight, and they have branches only at the crown, where sunlight falls. It is here that most of the photosynthesis takes place. In a way, the canopy is the "power plant" of the rain forest. We saw trees with leaves the size of dinner plates, and vines over 1,000 feet long.

> "I've been trying to spend time sitting quietly in the forest, hoping to learn more about some of the animals. There are several family groups of guenons here, so I hope that if I sit very still they might not notice me while they feed in a tree, leaping and running along the branches."

From the forest floor, the canopy above looked like a jungle of lacy branches and vines interlocked against the sky. In reality, it is a complicated network of roads and pathways upon which thousands of insects and other animals, large and small, travel. This maze of growth leads to spaces and hollows that provide homes for birds, mammals, reptiles, and amphibians.

Masters of Disguise

Chameleons are reptiles that live only in Africa and in parts of Asia and Europe. They are able to change their skin patterns and color in a matter of seconds in order to blend in with their surroundings. Some chameleons live beneath leaves on the forest floor, but most spend their lives in the trees. Tree-dwelling chameleons have smooth-soled feet, which they can wrap around branches.

FOUR-HORN CHAMELEON, CAMEROON

The Forest Strangler

"High in the canopy, a tiny, sticky fig seed lodges in the fork of a tree. The seed has probably been deposited there in the droppings of a monkey or bird that had fed on figs. The seed sprouts and begins to grow, sending pencil-thin roots down the side of the tree to the ground below.

Now that they have a stronghold in the soil, the roots grow and tangle around the trunk of the tree, competing with their host for nutrients. Back up in the canopy, fig leaves begin to grow quickly and soon rob the host tree of light. Meanwhile, the fig sends down more and more roots, putting pressure on its host, eventually choking off the tree's circulation.

Slowly, the strangler encircles the host tree, killing it. After the tree decomposes, what is left is a hollow tree-shaped form made up of the fig's tangled roots. It's true that these fig plants are stranglers—they kill trees—but they play an important role in the rain forest community. The hollow tree not only provides a home for many animals, it also provides a year-round supply of figs. The figs are food for many kinds of forest creatures."

More animals live in the canopy than in any other part of the forest. We could hear their calls, whistles, chirps, and grunts. And although we couldn't see them, we knew that the larger animals, such as squirrels and monkeys, swung and scampered along the rain forest "highway" with ease. We caught sight of some guenons, which are slender, graceful monkeys with long hind limbs, a long tail, and a rounded head. The name "guenon" comes from a French word for "fright." When these monkeys are startled or excited, they open their mouth as if they've been caught by surprise. Most guenons live in a family group in trees, where they forage primarily for fruit.

Over many millions of years, the plants and animals of the rain forest have adapted to their environment—and to each other—in many different ways. Monkeys have powerful limbs that they use to bridge the gaps between trees. By wrapping their strong tail around a tree branch, they free their hands for collecting and eating fruit, nuts, and insects. Some rain forest birds have developed short wings, allowing them to dart in and out of dense vegetation.

The Emergent Layer

The highest part of the forest is the emergent layer. Here the crowns of the tallest trees, which are shaped like open umbrellas, reach heights of up to 200 feet. These giant trees, along with the animals that live in them, get the full force of the sun and have adapted to the

Great Leapers

Moustached monkeys are found high in the canopy. They are great leapers, sometimes jumping as much as 60 feet between trees. In addition to insects, moustached monkeys feed on the fruits of many trees, including the oily fruit of palm trees.

MOUSTACHED MONKEY

dry conditions. Many trees have cup-shaped leaves to collect rainwater. Others have narrow, waxy leaves to hold in moisture, helping them resist the drying effects of the wind and the intense heat of the sun.

Standing on the forest floor, it was impossible to see many animals that lived in this highest layer of the forest. We knew, though, that there were birds and insects, spiders, and lizards—all adapted to the dry, windy conditions of "life at the top." Many of these animals lead their entire lives in the treetops without ever touching the ground.

Rain and the Rain Forest

Near the tops of many rain forest trees are small pools of water complete with tadpoles, lizards, and other small animals. Bromeliads, a type of epiphyte, are plants with stiff, waxy leaves arranged in a circular cluster. The cluster forms a "tank," and rainwater falls into it. Monkeys may

Canopy Daredevils

Most colobus monkeys have short thumbs or no thumbs at all, which is the reason for their name— "colobus" means "mutilated one." They are daredevils in the canopy, darting from tree to tree in death-defying leaps. Colobus monkeys are leaf-eaters, and their stomachs are specially adapted for digesting leaves and unripe fruit.

Right: A group of colobus monkeys.

EPIPHYTES

Epiphytes, or "air plants," have no attachment to the ground. They grow on trees or other plants for physical support and get water and minerals from rain and moisture in the air. Orchids and ferns are some of the most common species of epiphytes.

Above: Epiphytes in the rain forest. Right: Museum exhibit re-creation.

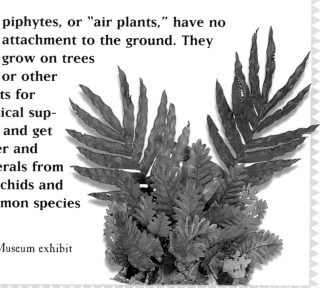

DEADLEAF
KATYDID, CONGO

C amouflage, or natural disguise, is just one of the many ways some rain forest animals have devised to fool predators. To hide from insect eaters, katydids and moths resemble twigs, leaves, or tree bark. Some butterflies use another strategy known as the "startle defense."

BUCKEYE
BUTTERFLY,
LIBERIA

When the butterfly's wings are closed, it looks like a dead leaf. But if a predator gets too close, the butterfly opens its richly colored wings. The flash of color may startle a predator and give the butterfly time to escape.

Camouflage is also used by predators in the hunt. The patterns on a snake's skin help it blend into its surroundings. In shadowy, dappled light the golden coat of a forest cat is a natural disguise.

LICHEN KATYDID, CAMEROON

Dazzling colors are frequently a warning that an animal is poisonous.

stop for a drink from a bromeliad, and some frogs deposit their eggs in these miniature wetlands.

While some plants hold water, others try to get rid of it. Rain forest plants often receive too much rainwater, and that can cause problems. Too much water on a plant can weigh it down, and constant wetness can cause decay. To get rid of excess water, many rain forest plants have developed slick-coated leaves with shapes that easily shed rain. Some even have spoutlike "drip tips" to help water drain quickly from the leaves' surfaces.

Come Here!

Many plants grow colorful, showy flowers with inviting scents to attract birds and insects. When the animal stops for a sip of nectar from the flowers, some pollen dust sticks to its body and is then passed on to the next flower the animal stops at. In this way, pollen is exchanged

Go Away!

Some animals use vivid colors as a warning to predators that they are poisonous. A bird that has eaten a bad-tasting brightly colored butterfly probably won't eat another one.

STINK BUG, CONGO

so that plants can make seeds that will grow into new plants.

Another method plants have to attract animals is growing fruit. Fruit is meant to be eaten, and this is the way many plants get animals to spread the plants' seeds. Tasty, sweet, usually colorful and nice smelling, fruit attracts animals. When a monkey or bird eats the fruit, the fruit's seeds pass through the animal's digestive system. The monkey moves on; the bird flies off. Later, the seeds are deposited in the animals' droppings, which provide fertilizer for the growing plant.

"Through the World Wildlife Fund, we hired a number of local people who helped us as guides, drivers, and trackers. They all greeted us and introduced themselves."

Much of the life of the rain forest was going on high above our heads. We could not see the birds whose songs rang through the forest, or the many millions of insects whose humming buzz seemed to surround us. There was a sense of unreality about being there—in the most complex and diverse ecosystem on earth.

1,000 Feet (Actually Only 710)

"Millipede" means "1,000 feet," but this animal never really has more than 355 pairs, or 710 feet. Some types of millipedes remain coiled and camouflaged, but if attacked give off an acid with a strong odor.

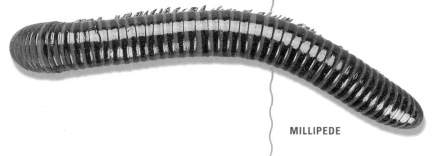

MILLIPEDE

A
Village
of
Elephants

▼▼▼▼▼
4

> **"The water was cool—and aah, the feel of elephant dung between your toes."**

Deep in the forest is the saline, or *bai*, as it is called in Sango. The saline is a natural forest floodplain, a watery marshland where elephants come to forage for the rich deposits of mineral salts that collect in the water. ("Saline" means "containing salt.")

We were all eager to see elephants, so we set off with our guide in a pick-up truck. Some of us rode in the back of the truck, holding on to the bars and ducking branches. As we traveled deeper into the forest, the vegetation thickened. Lianas, palms, and strangler figs grew together in a wild riot of green. Plants twisted up, around, over, and through each other in a crazy dance of growth. There was a dim glow of light overhead with only occasional shafts of sunlight breaking through the dense canopy made by the overarching trees.

> **"The air grew heavy, and the sounds of unseen animals and insects were all around us."**

Soon we had gone as far as we could in the truck, and we set off on foot, trudging single file through a maze of paths with our guide in the lead. Deeper

CHIMPANZEE

Forest Symphony

Click, hum, buzz, chirp, screech, hiss, squeal. The rain forest is alive with the sounds of thousands and thousands of insects, birds, and mammals.

and deeper into the forest we went. Animals we could hear, but not see, seemed to surround us. Birds in the understory squawked and called. There was a hum of insects and a distant, soft chattering of monkeys. Suddenly a chimpanzee, swinging on a liana vine, came crashing through the overhead growth. It may have been as startled as we were, for it let out a screaming shriek. Then, as quickly as it arrived, it disappeared, swinging back up into the trees, the leaves trembling in its wake.

Muck, Mud, and Elephant Dung

We reached one of the streams that feed the saline. Our guide warned us that the bottom of the stream was thick with mud so powerful it would suck the shoes right off our feet. So we

Don't Eat Me!

Predators stay away from net-wing beetles. Fluids produced in this beetle's body supposedly make them taste awful. Other insects mimic, or try to look like, net-wing beetles in order to avoid being eaten.

The Dzanga Bai, called "the village of elephants" by local people, is an open, marshy clearing 300 yards across and a half-mile long, surrounded by forest and fed by small streams.

Tusk marks can be seen on the ceiling of a cave that has been carved by elephants out of the soil. The forest is very poor in minerals, but here the soil is rich in calcium, something the elephants crave for bone and tusk growth. The elephants slide in on their front knees to eat the mineral-rich soil.

waded barefoot through the sometimes thigh-deep water for about a quarter of a mile. In some areas the mud was so deep it was a struggle to pull our feet out of it. When we did, the mud made a huge sucking sound.

On the far side of the stream we put on our shoes and headed through the forest again, following trails the elephants had made, the ground cover trampled flat by their huge feet.

Our guide cautioned us to be silent as we neared the saline. We crept quietly out of the gloom of the forest into the sunlit, watery clearing—and then we saw them. About 40 elephants—adults and their young—turned golden by the

Blowing for Salt

The elephants put their trunks into the water and blew bubbles to stir up the salt in the muddy bottom.

afternoon light on their mud-covered bodies. Digging and rooting, the elephants rolled and wallowed in the mineral-rich mud. Some hosed their backs with trunkfuls of gooey spray.

As we walked along the edge of the saline, the elephants picked up our scent. An alarm went out among them, and they ran to the far side of the saline. Slowly they spread out again, trunks in the air, checking the scent. The babies imitated their mothers' every move.

"Architects" of the Forest

Forest elephants look much like their savanna-dwelling cousins, but there are some differences. Forest elephants have smaller and more angular bodies. Their ears are also smaller and rounder, perhaps to make it easier for them to move through the thick forest growth. A forest elephant's tusks tend to be straighter and more slender than those of a savanna elephant.

Not much is known about the life of forest elephants. It is difficult to observe and study their behavior because of where they live. As large as

Not Just a Long Nose

An elephant uses its trunk to suck up water, about 2 gallons at a time, and empty it into its mouth. The trunk is incredibly flexible. There are no bones inside it, which is why an elephant can bend and curl it in any direction. At the end of the trunk there are two "fingers," which are so sensitive they can pick up a single leaf.

AFRICAN
FOREST
ELEPHANT

Elephants are the largest land-dwelling animals on earth, but they are among the gentlest. They eat only plants and become aggressive only when threatened.

Found in Africa and Asia, elephants are the only living members of the order Proboscidea, or "trunk bearers." Early elephant relatives included mammoths and mastodons, which became extinct about 10,000 years ago.

African savanna-dwelling elephants are the largest in the world. Asian elephants are slightly smaller, and African forest elephants are smaller still.

Little is known about forest elephants. Most information about elephants comes from observation and studies of those that live on the savanna. From them, researchers have learned that elephants travel in family groups, or herds. The leader of the herd is usually a grandmother, called a "matriarch." Females born into the herd may stay their whole lives, but the males usually leave the group between the ages of 8 and 20. After they leave, they travel alone or in small groups.

Elephants in a herd seem to be very affectionate. They snuggle, stand close together, touch each other, and intertwine their trunks.

	African Savanna Elephant	Asian Elephant	African Forest Elephant
Weight	7,125–13,000 pounds	9,000–12,000 pounds	7,000–9,000 pounds
Height	8–13 feet at the shoulder	8–10½ feet at the shoulder	6–8 feet at the shoulder
Appearance	back curves down in the middle; large, triangular ears; both males and females grow long tusks	back curves up in the middle; smaller, triangular ears; only males grow tusks long enough to be seen	rounded back; smaller, rounded ears; both males and females grow tusks

they are, the dense foliage of the rain forest keeps them well hidden, and, because they are able to tread quietly, the sound of their footsteps is nearly impossible to detect. Only here, at the saline, can they be easily observed.

But signs of elephants are found throughout the forest. They seem not to wander aimlessly, but to use the same routes over and over again, traveling alone or in small groups of up to four. Their trampled trails form networks that are also used by people and other animals. Elephant trails are much easier to follow than those made by people, who hack away the growth with a bush knife, leaving cut branches with sharp ends. The smoothly beaten-down paths of elephants often lead to fruit trees, for these animals will travel long distances in search of certain kinds of fruit in season.

Elephants are not picky eaters. Studies of savanna elephants show that an adult can eat up to 300 pounds of vegetation a day, including fruit, grasses, roots, vines, and the bark, branches, and leaves of trees.

In their search for food, elephants regularly redesign their surroundings, and much of what they do affects other animals and plants. We saw many trees with sections of bark missing—a sign that elephants had been there. They loosen the bark with their tusks and pull it off with their trunk. When they strip the bark from large trees, they rarely do

Walk Softly

An elephant puts its foot down starting with the tips of its toes. Its feet are constructed in such a way that the sole spreads out to take the weight of each step, and a spongy pad muffles the sound. That's why these huge animals can tread so softly through the forest. Except for the flapping of their ears, they hardly make any sound at all.

A Close Call

"I had climbed up on the viewing platform, and while I was there, our guides and the other team members took off—and then I saw why. Silently, swiftly, an elephant emerged from the forest.

It was too late; the platform was about 6 feet off the ground, and I couldn't get away.

The elephant passed not more than 30 feet in front of me. I tried to hide by crouching behind one of the saplings that served as a support for the platform. If I stood, I would be exactly at eye level with the elephant.

When the elephant was directly in front of me, it stopped, and so did my heart. I think it knew I was nearby but wasn't sure where. The elephant turned, standing in a typical threat posture. It probed the air with its trunk, looking for me. Suddenly it was not a magnificent wildlife sighting but a looming menace. After a few moments the elephant moved on as silently as it had arrived. From out of the forest, the other team members and the guides appeared. They all said how lucky I was."

lasting damage to them. But elephants do topple smaller trees, and they pull down branches by tugging on vines. This opens up a clearing in the forest where light can reach the forest floor. New plants begin to grow, and their tender leaves are eaten by gorillas and forest antelopes.

Spreading seeds is another important role of elephants in the forest. By eating a variety of different fruits, elephants carry the seeds of plants to new areas, where they can grow yet not compete with the parent plant. The sturdy seeds of plants pass through the elephant's digestive system and are deposited in the dung, which acts as an instant fertilizer.

On Location

We returned to the saline a number of times. One of the most difficult trips was when those of us on the film crew went to photograph the elephants. We wanted some footage of both evening and early morning, so we decided to spend the night, camping out on the thatched-roof viewing platform on the edge of the saline. It was never easy to reach the saline, but sloshing and slogging through the muddy tracts with all the heavy camera equipment made the trip twice as difficult.

On the way there, we went into a clearing where some buffalo were feeding on grasses. We moved toward them to get a better shot, but when we did, we sank into the mud.

We twisted around, trying to get our footing and help pull each other out, but we only sank deeper. Finally we managed to hand the equipment to the guide and fling ourselves forward onto dry ground. A few feet ahead was a clear stream, where we

Bush Cows

Forest buffalo, or "bush cows," are smaller than the buffalo found on the African savanna. Their horns are not as large, and their coats are a reddish color rather than the black of their savanna relatives. They do, however, like the same diet of grasses.

A group of four
elephants makes
its way through
a patch of giant
lobelia plants.

BEETLE
AND
DUNG BALL

There are thousands of species of dung beetles. Seeking out the droppings of larger animals such as elephants and gorillas, some dung beetles roll a chunk of dung into a Ping-Pong-sized ball. Some beetles then build a chamber below the ball, while others roll it away to an underground tunnel. The female beetle may lay eggs inside the balls. When the eggs hatch, the larvae will feed on the dung while the nutrients in the buried dung balls help enrich the soil and fertilize plants.

Other types of dung beetles don't bother to roll the droppings—they simply tunnel into the dung to feed on it or to lay their eggs in it. Still others are dung ball thieves! They steal the balls rolled by other beetles.

"ROLLING"
DUNG BEETLE

"TUNNELING"
DUNG
BEETLES

Some types of butterflies feed on the droppings of meat-eaters, such as leopards. Rich in salt, the droppings help butterflies keep the correct balance of minerals in their systems.

knelt to try to clean ourselves off. After all that, we didn't get any good shots of those buffalo!

When we finally reached the saline, we set up our cameras, but a storm was moving in. There was little light, which made filming impossible, and the equipment was sensitive to the humidity.

Suddenly the sky went black. We were standing on the platform overlooking the darkness. Lightning would strike, and for an instant we could see the entire saline with elephants all over the place. Then darkness again.

> "Since we couldn't do any filming, we went to sleep early. One of the crew started snoring. He was really loud, and a bull elephant began to respond. When the snore changed timbre, so did the elephant. I wish I had taped it!"

Sometime during the night, an elephant came under the platform where we were sleeping to scratch itself on one of the posts. It shook the whole place like a mini-earthquake, and we all sat up. The next morning, we saw the elephant's footprints around the post.

Everyone on the team learned a few lessons about elephants. Mainly, we learned to respect them—and their territory.

Road Builders

Elephants are natural bulldozers. The trails they make are much smoother than the ones made by people.

People Versus Elephants

The ivory of elephant tusks has long been prized around the world. Its hard, shiny white surface has made it a favorite material for sculptures, jewelry, billiard balls, piano keys, and much more. Because of people's desire for ivory, elephants were being hunted to near extinction. Between 1981 and 1989, the population of African

ELEPHANT DUNG BEETLE, ACTUAL SIZE

elephants decreased from 1,190,000 to 622,000. People realized that elephants needed to be protected. In 1989, 130 countries around the world agreed to ban all trade in ivory. Now more elephants are being born and more are surviving, and this is causing a different kind of problem.

Elephants have an obvious majesty, beauty, and intelligence, but for the people who share the forest with them, these 5-ton creatures that flatten their fences, wipe out their farm harvests, and endanger their children can be a serious problem.

New solutions, such as electrified fences around fields, show promise for protecting crops from intruding elephants. Finding ways for people and animals to live together in the rain forest is one of the goals of the Dzanga-Sangha conservation project.

"Elephants have incredible memories and pass knowledge on to the next generation. They associate humans with death, so they usually run if they pick up the scent of people. If an elephant is threatened, it will charge. We were told to always know where the nearest, biggest tree was so we could run behind it."

Monster Fruit

Some rain forest plants, such as *pomba*—a liana with fruit that looks like yellow cannonballs—may depend solely on elephants to spread their seeds. The *pomba* shells are as hard as rocks and are more than half an inch thick. Only an elephant, with its powerful jaws, could crack such a monstrous shell to get to the fruit—and the seeds—inside it.

GREEN BUSH VIPER

"In film school I used to dream of making films in the wilds. Well, here I am. I guess my dream came true."

We were all eager to start working. We had only 6 weeks to collect everything we needed, and there was a lot to do. Different teams went their own way, some collecting plants, trees, and vines, others studying mammals or birds or insects. The film crew, artists, and photographers were responsible for recording all the visual references we would need to re-create the look of the forest. We had the designers' plans and drawings for the exhibit. Now it was up to us to collect the things they would need to build it.

The type of lifelike, life-size exhibit we would create is known as a diorama—a three-dimensional scene that gives the viewer a feeling of what it's like to actually be in a particular place. In this case, of course, it was the Dzanga-Sangha rain forest.

Most dioramas have a painted background. The Dzanga-Sangha diorama, however, would have a "video wall," a constantly running film that would serve as a backdrop for

On location in the rain forest, two members of the film crew set up a shot.

the exhibit. It would show the animals in their habitat—elephants at the saline, birds taking flight through the trees. The video's sound track would make the exhibit even more realistic. Visitors would be able to hear the chattering of monkeys, the calls of birds, and the trumpeting of elephants. A quick rustle among the tangled growth might indicate a bird coming

CICADA

"The sound track on the video was a loud symphony of forest sounds—cicada rasps, bird trills, and the steady hoots of monkeys. When amplified, it sounded like a rock band."

to nest or perhaps a gorilla or chimpanzee moving through the trees. In order to do this, we would need many hours of film and tape.

How to Walk Through a Rain Forest

With the help of the guides, we began scouting locations to film. We had to train ourselves to walk through the forest and really "see" it. We were well aware that we were the guests here. For many of us, the rain forest was the most beautiful natural area we had ever seen, but this was the animals' realm, and we depended on our guides' intimate knowledge of the animals and their territory.

As we trekked through the forest, our guide would occasionally signal us to stop. We'd all freeze. Listen. Look. An elephant would move through the forest into a clearing; a duiker antelope would come in answer to our guide's call, then take off when it saw us. We were learning to sharpen our senses— to see what at first seemed invisible, to hear the life here.

Giant Web Sites

Certain types of spiders, called "social spiders," live and work together in huge, interlocked webs. When insects such as cockroaches and grasshoppers are caught in the webs, a pack of spiders overpowers and devours them.

SOCIAL SPIDER

While the film crew scouted shooting locations, those of us on the collecting team also walked the forest, selecting sites to replicate for the exhibit. We had long lists of the things we would need—a termite mound, a chimpanzee nest, a giant rat burrow, and many kinds of ferns, vines, and trees.

"I was walking along a tiny footpath that might have been the remains of an old elephant trail, trying to remember how the BaAka taught me to put each foot before the next so as to make the least noise and not disturb any animals."

We organized everything by drawing maps of different forest areas, then dividing them into grids and numbering them. That way, we'd know where to find a certain tree or nest again.

After selecting the sites we wanted to copy, our artists sketched and did watercolor studies of the leaves, flowers, vines, and roots. We took thousands of photographs to record every detail—the position of birds' nests, the way a vine twisted around a tree, the delicate patterns formed by mosses growing on tree trunks.

Leaf 193

Using orange plastic markers, we tagged the trees and vines we would later cut down and remove from the forest.

Left: Color studies of leaves and trees would help the artists re-create them at the Museum many months later.

Right: A BaAka man scales a tree with the aid of a vine.

Insect Drive-In

"Some of the best places to find insects, spiders, and centipedes were in small bodies of water. Hundreds might settle in a puddle, and we'd just sneak up and grab them.

But our favorite method of collecting insects was night-hunting at the airport. Near sunset, a group of us met at the airstrip with collecting jars, flashlights, and folding chairs. We set up a large white sheet across the runway, and behind the sheet we put a bright light. It looked as if we were at a drive-in movie, waiting for the projectionist to crank up the film.

The light of the lantern attracted many moths and other small insects. As they settled onto the sheet, we gently scooped them into collecting jars. We gathered hundreds of insects this way.

Knowing that different parts of the forest and different times of the night would bring out different kinds of insects, we planned on setting up elsewhere next week."

One large type of centipede is called *Alipes*, or wing-foot, because of the shape of its hind legs, which are so flat and thin they resemble wings. As this centipede walks, it raises these unusually shaped legs into the air and waves them to and fro. The fanning motion creates a whispering sound, which may distract or ward off potential predators.

With the help of local workers, we cut down the trees, plants, and vines we had tagged earlier. It was hard work, and we wouldn't have been able to do it without the local people. We watched in amazement as they scaled a 50-foot tree with only the aid of a vine wrapped around their waist, the other end secured to the trunk of the tree. They carried a knife in their mouth when they climbed to cut epiphytes, which grew high in the branches of the tree.

Buzzing, Biting, and Bothersome

Plant collecting might sound like an easy job, but it wasn't. The forest was hot and humid, and we were constantly pestered by little buzzing bees known as "sweat" bees. They didn't bite or sting but were attracted by moisture— namely, our sweat. The sheer numbers crawling on our necks, faces, eyes, noses, and ears and in our mouths drove us a bit crazy. We couldn't help but inhale some of them, which was pretty awful— but the ants were even worse.

"I was cutting down a tree when a shower of ants came raining down on me. They got inside my shirt and crawled under my pants legs. They bite, and while holding on, bring their abdomen around to administer venom with a stinger. Wow—did they ever hurt!"

We had never seen anything quite like the huge colonies of driver ants. In groups that can number over 20 million, they march through the forest like a gigantic army. Soldier ants stand guard at the edges of the column with their big jaws open wide. They protect their troops and are ready to do battle with any intruders. Careful not to get in their way, we watched a column 20 feet long

Sweat and Blood

Sweat bees are attracted to the sweat of people and animals because of the salt it contains. Another persistent rain forest pest is the horsefly. It will attack and bite any kind of animal to obtain a blood meal for itself and its young.

HORSEFLY

and 6 inches wide move through the area where we were working.

Although driver ants do no serious harm to people, they attack if they are disturbed. They have a vicious bite and won't let go. When that happens, a person might be seen running through the forest to escape. As we found out, "ants in your pants" can be a real problem, and people had to quickly strip off some of their clothes to get rid of ants clinging to their skin.

Driver ants' main prey are other insects, millipedes, and spiders, which they swarm over and eat alive. They also consume small mammals and reptiles. Lizards and even large snakes aren't safe from driver ants. The swarm can move at the rate of about 65 feet an hour, and any animals in its

A dried leaf from the forest and one plaster "leaf cookie" made from a similar leaf.

Making "Leaf Cookies"

Behind the lodge was a large building we turned into a workshop for making "leaf cookies." We would carefully apply a thin layer of plaster of Paris to the top side of each leaf, which would record the details. We would then add more layers of plaster to build up the thickness and "strength" of the "cookies."

PAINTING A LEAF

The plaster casts would later be used to make vacuum-molded plastic leaves for the exhibit. Real leaves, of course, would shrivel and die. But with our "leaf cookies" we would be able to make exact duplicates to attach to the vines and trees we would also be making from casts and molds.

path—if they don't move out of the way—can be overtaken and devoured.

Driver ants have been known to march through people's homes in the villages, rather like a tropical rain forest exterminating crew. The residents know it's best to leave until the ants have moved out. They won't harm the house, but they will eat any mice or insects they find there.

Some kinds of driver ants form a nest in a hollow tree or underground. For others, the nest is the tightly clumped bodies of the ants themselves.

> "Even though I covered myself with insect repellent, I got over 50 bites. I give up."

Inhaling bees and being bitten by ants came with the job of collecting. We tried hard not to let it bother us too much as we bundled and labeled leaves and small branches and vines. Some plants were labeled and put in the herbarium press, which dries and preserves them. Some were put in plastic bags for color studies, and others were placed in glycerine and formalyn solution buckets for preservation.

Other members of the crew drew or photographed trees and leaves, while still others gathered

Jaws

The mandibles, or jaws, of driver ants are so strong that some people in the forest use them to close wounds. They place an ant over the wound so that it will bite it on both sides. The body of the ant is then pinched off and the head is left in place. The ant's jaws stay shut, keeping the wound closed until it heals.

Some leaves were put into a herbarium press, which dries and preserves them.

TERMITES ON THE FOREST FLOOR

Inside the termite mound there is constant activity. The mound can be home to many thousands of termites, and each has a job. Every colony has a queen, soldiers, and workers.

The queen is the only one in the colony who can lay eggs. She might live to be 15 years old, and she lays hundreds of thousands of eggs in her lifetime. In her chamber, the queen termite is surrounded by workers tending to her. They feed her, clean her, and look after the eggs until they develop into adult termites.

Outside the entrance of the mound, a termite soldier might use its large jaws to attack enemies or intruders, such as ants.

Inside the mound, the tunnels are filled with streams of busy workers. Some leave the mound to gather food for the colony. Others help take care of the queen or the eggs.

How to Eat a Termite

First, select the large soldiers and pinch their heads to kill them. Then, pop them in your mouth. They have a slight almond flavor and make a good trailside snack.

Workers tend to the queen, whose head appears in the upper left corner. It is obvious from this picture that the queen is hundreds of times larger than the other termites in the colony.

dried leaf litter from the forest floor or made impressions, called "texture stamps," of tree bark, which would be used to fabricate trees for the Museum's exhibit.

Recycling the Rain Forest

Everything in the forest had an intense feeling of life—even the forest floor, where vast swarms of termites made loud humming and crunching sounds as they ate.

Termites are social insects that live in large colonies. Some colonies are underground, but many are towering mounds of soil standing as tall as 30 feet high. In the process of building their mounds, termites mix soil layers and redistribute organic matter.

Termites play another key role by helping to recycle the nutrients in the forest. They are important decomposers of plants and are constantly cleaning the forest by feeding on dead and dying plant material. Termites are able to digest wood, which changes to sugar inside their bodies. In turn, many animals, including people, eat termites, which are rich in calories.

We found some termite mounds that had been crushed and broken into—undoubtedly the work of aardvarks or pangolins. "Aardvark" means "earth pig," and it is a good name for this animal that spends most of its time digging under-

"With the help of our guides, I collected some termites and driver ants. I watched them carefully in case they ate their way out of the bags we'd put them in. I also had the strange task of collecting a bagful of bongo droppings—now, how often can you say that!"

Insect Architects

Termites are master builders, and the mounds they create have elaborate tunnels, entrances, and exits. These well-built nests can withstand heavy rainfall and water dripping down from the canopy overhead.

LONG-HORN BEETLE

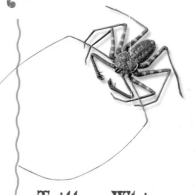

ground for ants or termites. Using its sensitive snout, it locates a termite nest, then breaks it open with its large, powerful claws. The aardvark then sucks up the termites with its sticky 12-inch-long tongue.

With every day that passed, we became more attuned to the forest and the animals. We began to recognize the calls of many creatures and, with the help of our guides, even learned to make some calls ourselves. We became more aware of the signs an animal leaves behind, such as broken termite mounds and discarded fruit. We also began to identify specific animals' tracks and dung. By observing things firsthand, we reached a deeper understanding of how all life in the forest is inter-connected.

Meanwhile, our collecting work was going well, and a small mountain of the future diorama began to pile up by the side of the road.

Tailless Whip Scorpion

While its name sounds fierce, the tailless whip scorpion is quite harmless. Only about 1 inch in length, it can make itself look as much as 3 times bigger by extending its legs outward.

PANGOLINS

Pangolins, or scaly anteaters, are covered with overlapping scales. The adults range in size from 1 to 3 feet long, plus a tail that is the same length as the body. Like aardvarks, they locate termite mounds by smell and use their long, wormlike tongues to get at their prey. The name "pangolin" means "rolling over," referring to this animal's habit of curling into a ball when threatened.

People
of the
Rain Forest

6

> ## "The land does not belong to us, we belong to the land."

Over thousands of years, many different ethnic groups have settled in the Dzanga-Sangha area. Peoples such as the Ngundi fished along the Sangha River. Some Bantu-speaking groups formed villages and cleared land to grow food such as sweet potatoes and manioc, while the BaAka people hunted forest animals for meat and gathered many kinds of forest plants for food, medicines, and building materials. Although today most people farm or work in the lumber mill or with the conservation project, all still depend on the natural resources of the forest.

Like their ancestors before them, the BaAka rely heavily on hunting and gathering for their daily needs.

> "When the BaAka need something such as nets, baskets, or ropes, they make it from the plants they find in the forest. When they are finished using whatever it is they've made, they throw it away. Very practical, very basic."

Hunters

The point of a BaAka hunting spear was made by a village blacksmith. A length of *kpongbo* may serve as the handle for the spear, and string made from a *kosa* plant was used to attach the spear point to the handle.

KOSA

Hunting raises complicated issues for conservation. All forms of hunting are illegal in Dzanga-Ndoki National Park. Yet people have to eat. Forest animals such as porcupine and duikers are the main source of protein for most BaAka, and traditional hunting with handmade traps and nets is permitted in the Dzanga-Sangha Reserve. Many BaAka trade or sell some of the plants and animals they collect.

Plants for Food, Medicine, and Housing

Auguste, one of our guides, agreed to lead us on a rain forest walk to show us plants for everything from making a hut to curing a stomachache. He brought his entire family—his

GAO

The stems of *gao* are used to weave mats and baskets.

Ferns reproduce by dispersing chalk-like spores from the undersides of their leaves. The spores are distributed by wind and rain.

mother, two wives, eight children, aunts, and cousins along for the walk. Some other BaAka women joined us too, so it was quite a party that set off into the forest that day.

Auguste showed us a colorful tree called *malanga*, the sap of which runs red when the trunk is cut. *Malanga* bark is used to make medicine, while the trunk and wood are used to make boats and oars.

With a sharp knife, Auguste made a cut in a large, grooved vine. He made a second cut lower on the vine, and then cut the vine into several shorter pieces. He handed each of us a section of vine, telling us to tip it up and drink from it. The vine was filled with water!

> "The BaAka language has only about 3,000 words and all the verbs are in present tense."

"It is called *nzambi*," Auguste said, "the water vine."

Gao is solid, light, and easy to find. The spiny thorns of the *gao* plant must be removed before the stems can be split and woven into mats, Auguste explained, and large woven mats make sturdy beds. The plant is also used to make small, flat baskets to carry meat or fish. A length of *gao* can be used to mix bowls of manioc, to make a rattle for a baby, or even to make a flute.

The women showed us several kinds of plants used to make baskets. *Kpongbo* is a flexible vine

Gatherers

The BaAka collect nuts, fruit, mushrooms, honey, and caterpillars as well as many plants for food, medicine, and building materials. They are knowledgeable about which roots will yield poison for their hunting arrows and which leaves will cure a snakebite.

Vines such as *nzambi*, or "water vine," are among several plants that produce drinkable water in the forest. Vines like this one allow the BaAka to make camps far from running water. Rain forests are abundant in moisture, partly because plants are excellent absorbers of water, but it isn't always easy to find rivers or streams in the forest.

without thorns on its stem. The vines are pulled from the ground and brought back to the campsite. There they are cut, split into sections, and scraped with a sharp knife until they are supple enough to weave into a basket. *Kpongbo* is also used to make boxes to carry honey.

Kosa, a very common plant, has fan-shaped leaves and "hairy" stems that can cause painful scratches. Auguste explained that after the "hair" is stripped from the stem, *kosa* is used to make rope, hunting nets, traps, belts, and ankle bracelets. It is also used for the string on a bow or to attach spear

MBATEMA

The leaves of *mbatema* are used to make a medicine to cure snakebites.

How to Get Honey

"The first thing to do is find a beehive. It is usually hidden high, high up in the trees—sometimes 100 feet up. Watch and listen for bees buzzing. When there is a swarm of bees, make a **nzambi** vine into a belt to grip around the tree for climbing. While the belt is being readied, someone else makes a fire; another person makes a basket out of vines. Use the baked leaves of **kosa** plants to cover the face to prevent bee stings. The first person to climb carries the embers of the fire wrapped in leaves. He blows smoke into the nest and enlarges the opening. Bees fly out. Another person climbs the tree and comes to help. Together they scoop out the honey, put it in the basket, and lower it to the people waiting on the ground. Everyone is waiting for the honey."

points to a stick. Making rope is usually a man's job, and it can take months of work to braid and weave enough rope for a big hunt.

Auguste plucked a large leaf off a *koko* vine. "*Koko* is similar to salad, and a source of nourishment, " he said. "After being cut into thin strips, the leaves of *koko* are cooked." One of the women added that *koko* leaves are much sought after by many people outside the forest, and they are frequently traded for manioc or other cultivated food.

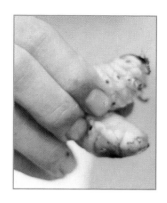

> "Auguste kept offering me the grubs, or larvae, of beetles. They looked like tiny raw shrimp. 'Try one,' he'd say, eating a handful. 'Think of them as jungle sushi,' someone on our team suggested, but I couldn't bring myself to eat them."

Jungle Sushi

At certain times of the year when fish and game are scarce, protein is hard to come by. Forest people eat caterpillars and beetle larvae, which are highly nutritious.

When the BaAka are traveling through the rain forest without pots or cooking utensils, they place mushrooms and a bit of meat on a *koko* leaf, roll it up, and cook it over a fire in a packet of heavier, thicker leaves called *ngongo*.

The large *ngongo* leaf has many uses. Twisted into a spiral, it can be used as a funnel. Folded, it becomes a drinking cup. One leaf can serve as a plate, or a fan to stoke a fire. Several leaves together make a baby's sun hat.

With a machete, one of the women began cutting down young *bemba* trees. After stripping the bark, she drove the saplings into the ground to form a circle and then wove the top ends of the trees together in a dome shape. She covered the armature with *ngongo* leaves, overlapping them to make a sturdy, rain-resistant hut.

The BaAka word for the rubber tree is *landa*. Auguste demonstrated how the rubber flows from

NGONGO

MANIOC

One of the most important food plants is manioc, or cassava. A shrubby plant with brittle stems, large, palm-like leaves, and green flowers, it grows 6 to 8 feet high. It is from this plant's huge, tuberous root, which can weigh up to 30 pounds, that cassava flour is made. In many tropical locations, where starchy foods are hard to come by, manioc is a food staple. In addition to flour, manioc root is used to make bread, soup, and a sweet paste that is spread on stone griddles and cooked over a fire. It does, however, take a lot of work to prepare—and that's because of the poison.

The first person who tried manioc must have been very clever or was soon very dead, because it is not easy to get rid of the toxic liquid. The root must be sliced, grated, washed, and pressed to remove the poison.

the tree when the bark is cut. *Landa* is used to make balls and tops. To make a ball, thin layers of the rubber are spread out to dry. The dried sheet of rubber is then wrapped around a ball of soil. More and more layers of dried rubber are added until the ball is the desired thickness. A hole is then made in the ball, the soil is poured out, and the hole is plugged with a small piece of rubber.

Auguste pointed out a shrub called *sombolo*. A medicine to kill chigger fleas, which burrow into people's feet, is made from the roots of this plant. The leaves of *sombolo* are also useful. Instead of a

Swifty

Agama lizards, sometimes running only on their back feet, are capable of high-speed chases in pursuit of ants, termites, and beetles, on which they feed. These 14-inch-long lizards can also scamper up walls and rocks with ease. Agama lizards make their homes in cliffs and rock crevices.

AGAMA LIZARDS

feather, a *sombolo* leaf is inserted into a slit at the end of an arrow. The arrows themselves are made from the stalks of a *raphia* palm known as *bungu*. The stalks are split into long, thin sections and one end is sharpened into a point with a knife.

One of the women picked up a *ngemba* twig from the forest floor. "It is used to brush teeth," Auguste explained. "And sometimes it is added to sauces because it has a nice smell."

Women's Work

We couldn't help but notice that the women did most of the gardening and plant collecting. They carried their babies with them as they dug sweet potatoes and collected wild fruit.

They were also the ones who did most of the fishing. At times of the year when there is less rain and the water levels are low, the BaAka women travel to forest streams and areas along the river. There they dig canals and make dams with branches and mud to lower the water level even further.

"The women do all the housework, harvest the manioc, and gather wood. They carry bundles of wood on their heads that I couldn't even lift."

Using cups, shells, or simply their hands, they scoop up shrimp, crabs, and several kinds of fish including a spiny-backed catfish. The women wrap the fish in *ngongo* leaves and cook the packets over an open fire. When the leaves begin to burn, they know the fish is cooked.

Another form of cooking involves heating stones in a fire and then placing the food on large leaves set on top of the hot stones.

Rain Forest Makeup

BaAka girls and women use the seeds of the *ndemba* plant to produce a black liquid. They then use the liquid to paint geometric patterns on their forehead and cheeks. This makeup lasts several days.

NDEMBA

Butterfly larvae, or caterpillars, feed on a leaf in the rain forest.

New Ways of Life

Many BaAka work for the logging company or on the plantations of Bantu-speaking people. Some, such as the guides and helpers who have worked with us, are being trained through the conservation program and receive better pay than those who work for loggers or on other people's plantations. Some BaAka are also clearing parts of the forest for their own farm plots. We have much to learn from these people of the forest, for their knowledge of plants and the workings of the forest have been passed down for hundreds of generations.

> "I have a deep respect for the knowledge of the BaAka. They are the experts here—on the terrain, the animals, and the uses of plants."

KOKO

Deep
Forest
Site

▼▼▼▼▼▼▼

7

"The camp was located on a hill overlooking the river."

Four of us on the collecting team set up camp deep in the forest, 5 miles away from Doli Lodge. It was a beautiful site, located where the Sangha and the smaller Babongo River meet. Used as a safari camp, there were several small buildings, one of which we had access to. We used it as a work-house and pitched tents on high ground near the river to sleep in. There was also one small house where the BaAka family who act as caretakers for the safari camp lived.

> "As soon as I saw light through my tent, I hurried outside to catch the sunrise and watch the birds flying over the river. But the river also reflects light from the moon and stars, and the sun was not yet rising. It was only 3:00 A.M."

The father of the family was the local chief. He was very formal, polite and dignified, greeting us warmly as he went off in the morning to tend to business, often not coming back for days. His eldest son stayed at the lodge with his wife and children, as did his youngest son, Victor, who was 14. Victor usually walked the 2 miles to school in Bayanga, but while we were there he was allowed

A Rain Forest Backpack

The BaAka people weave baskets from rain forest plants. The baskets are worn like back-packs, but instead of two shoulder straps there is a single strap that loops around the head.

to play hooky to help us. Mostly he helped bait and tend the traps set out for small mammals, such as mice and rats, and for snakes and frogs.

Our camp was on a fairly well-traveled forest path, and every now and then people would pass through. One day a group of BaAka came by carrying large baskets of *ngongo* leaves that they had collected in the forest. Small domed huts would be made watertight by overlapping the large heart-shaped leaves.

BaAka hunters also passed through late one morning. Victor spoke with them, and he translated for us. They told him they were on their way to a certain part of the forest to hunt porcupine.

Bright Feathers and Bold Beaks

With the help of our guides we set up mist nets—special equipment used by ornithologists to study birds. The birds fly into the fine netting, which does not hurt them, but they are trapped. We made a map of all the locations, and then we put numbers on the nets so that when we freed the birds, we would know which nets they came from. Some of the nets were deep in the forest, some in natural clearings, some in the openings on the riverbank, and others in the flooded forest formed by the Babongo River.

Feathery Predator

The African crowned eagle has a wingspan of 6 feet. It preys on forest animals as large as monkeys and duiker antelopes.

Great blue turacos build nests on flimsy platforms of twigs high in the tallest trees of the canopy. Because turaco chicks leave the nest after only 4 weeks or so, they don't need a bigger or sturdier home.

Soon after first light, we made our daily rounds to check the mist nets. We gently removed the birds that had flown into the nets and examined them. We kept records of all the birds—identifying and describing them in our journals, keeping track of which nets they were found in. We measured them, photographed them, and cataloged them. There are more than 300 species of birds in this African rain forest. Many have fantastic coloring or unusually shaped beaks.

We watched a flock of great blue turacos—large birds with bright violet-blue feathers and long tails—as they fed in the trees. They flew or climbed

Mealtime

Many rain forest birds feed on insects such as flies, ants, termites, and moths.

AFRICAN GREY PARROTS

Of all birds, African grey parrots are considered to be the best "talkers." They are able to imitate the whistle of a teapot, the meow of a cat, and human speech. Until recently, it was assumed that parrots could only imitate the sounds of words, but scientists are discovering that African grey parrots can be trained to attach meanings to those sounds.

Irene Pepperberg, a scientist who has spent 20 years studying animal behavior, has trained two African grey parrots to count; identify over 30 objects by name, shape, and color; and understand such concepts as same and different.

According to Pepperberg, it is logical that parrots, which live in social groups, can learn to communicate. In their rain forest habitat, it is difficult to see through the dense vegetation, and they have probably developed complex vocal signals to stay in touch with one another.

Because of their popularity as pets, the total number of parrots in the wild has dropped dramatically. In 1981, parrots were placed on the threatened species list, and it became illegal to capture them.

GIANT
KINGFISHER

TRUMPETER
HORNBILL

Most hornbills make their nest in hollow trees. When the female has laid the eggs, she sits on them while the male hornbill brings mud and other material to seal up the entrance hole in the tree. A small slit is left in the mud through which the male can feed the female while she is sitting on the eggs. After the chicks have hatched, the mud is broken away to free the mother bird. The hole may then be sealed up again, except for a slit through which the youngsters will be fed until they are strong enough to leave the nest. Throughout the whole nesting and hatching process, first the eggs and then the young have been protected from predators.

Hornbills live in flocks, unlike kingfishers, which are solitary birds. Despite their name, most kingfishers eat land animals such as lizards, spiders, and insects, rather than fish. Kingfishers nest in holes in riverbanks or in termite mounds.

PYGMY
KINGFISHER

RED-BILLED
DWARF HORNBILL

CASQUED HORNBILL

nimbly from branch to branch much like monkeys, eating fruits and berries. Most turacos travel in pairs or occasionally in groups of up to 12 birds.

The most impressive beaks were those of the hornbills. Their large and usually brightly colored, downward-curving bills take many forms. Some are like pincers, perfect for collecting fruit and eating seeds. Others have a double horny cap on the top, near the head. We frequently heard the hornbills' loud, croaking voices and the whistling sound their wings made as they flew from tree to tree.

We also saw many types of kingfishers. Holding its prey in its beak, the bird beats it against its perch to kill it. The kingfisher may then toss its meal up into the air before swallowing it. The colorful, shining blue kingfisher has a peacock-like fan of

Mud-Stirrer

Shuffling along streams and rivers, the hamerkop, or hammer-headed stork, stirs up mud to raise mollusks, frogs, and small fish, which it feeds on. These 2-foot-long wading birds build enormous nests— some as large as 6 feet across and 4 feet wide.

Stirring up mud along a riverbank, a hamerkop hunts its prey.

Victor

"Sometimes Victor would come with me to check the mist nets. He was very attuned to hearing animals, and he would gesture wildly and cup his ear to alert us to a sound. We hadn't heard a thing, but we would listen intently when he told us to. It usually turned out to be a very far-off monkey.

Victor had a wonderful chicken coop that he built himself. It was about 3 feet off the ground, with a ladder for the chickens and a wide thatched roof. The chickens don't look like our chickens at all. They're shaped differently and are far more colorful. They're very streamlined, with no fat. They put their heads down and then straight out, and then they **run**!

Victor showed me a line of snare traps he'd set. He hoped to catch a small animal that he says raids his chicken coop. We think maybe it's a mongoose.

While we were working, Victor liked to sit and draw. He drew some animals and named them for me. He also drew from my field guides. While he worked, I talked to him about biology and science, but he said he was interested in becoming a diamond miner."

black and blue plume feathers, a fire-engine red beak, and a purple "cape."

From time to time we caught a bright flash of the metallic green feathers of a sunbird or heard the "cheeps" and "ticks" of their squeaky, trilling song.

Occasionally we would stop our work and stand still and silent, listening to the sounds of the forest and the flowing river. Golden shafts of light made their way through gaps in the treetops, forming angled, misty beams in the warm, moist air.

"Today I got up at 5:00 A.M., just before the parrots started their day. Soon they were overhead, sounding their complicated flight calls of whistles, screeches, and musical whoops. For 3 hours there were parrots in the sky—so many pairs and groups of 3 that I soon lost count. Some of them flew quite close to me because I was perched on top of the riverbank. It was as if they were flying across the river toward me."

Flying Pests

There was no electricity in the workhouse, and it was dark by 6:00 P.M., so every daylight hour counted. We used gas lanterns to work at night, but their light was so bright that it attracted hordes of tiny green flies that fit perfectly through the screen around the workhouse. At first we solved this problem by taping black plastic trash bags over the screens, but that made the room too hot. Later we wore headlamps—bands that fit around our heads, with a light attached in front. That caused another kind of problem. Moths and flying termites were attracted to the light, and they flew into our faces. After a while, we got used to it.

The Suspect

A mongoose is a small mammal about the size and shape of a ferret. Mongooses feed mainly on rats, lizards, worms, and insects. Some eat fruit, and many are fond of eggs, which they take between their front feet and smash against the ground to break open the shell.

At night we crawled into our tents and unzipped the roof panels so we could gaze at the stars. The ground was hard, and there were lots of insects, especially small red beetles that found their way into our tents and sleeping bags.

"The only thing between me and the wildest birds and animals is this thin piece of nylon tent. Leopards, elephants, bongos, gorillas, and chimpanzees might cross my path. If I stop to think about it, it's kind of scary. But right now I'd rather be here than anywhere else in the world."

As we drifted off to sleep, we could hear the sounds of the nocturnal animals. Strange whoops and calls echoed through the forest. One of the eeriest sounds was the high-pitched, wailing cry of the tree hyrax, which sounded like someone being strangled. Some evenings we heard a BaAka woman singing her baby to sleep. The song she sang was beautiful, rich, and complex. We never tired of hearing it.

Ear-Splitter

The hyrax is a noisy little animal that looks a bit like a guinea pig but is—amazingly—related to elephants. Tree hyraxes spend the day sleeping in holes in trees and come out at night to feed. Before entering or leaving a tree, they call to signal their presence. The call begins as soft groaning and rises to an ear-splitting shriek that can be heard up to a mile away. Tree hyraxes are excellent climbers, and descend from their homes in the trees to feed on leaves, fruit, grass, and ferns. In the trees, they seek out insects, lizards, and birds' eggs.

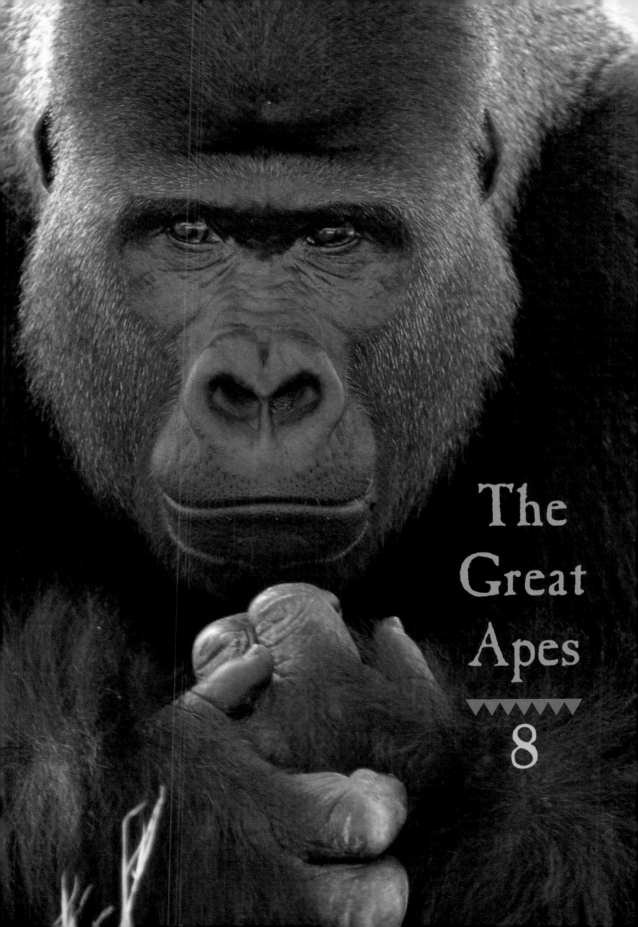

The
Great
Apes

8

"Never look a gorilla in the eye."

There are perhaps 7,000 to 8,000 lowland gorillas in the Dzanga-Sangha rain forest, but we'd be lucky to catch sight of just one. Secretive and elusive, these great apes are difficult to find, for they are almost always on the move and leave few signs of where they've been.

In 1988, zoologist Dr. Richard Carroll set up a research center in Dzanga-Sangha to study lowland gorillas. With the help of BaAka guides, he tracked gorillas to find out how they live and travel through the rain forest. Dr. Carroll offered to take us on a gorilla-tracking expedition. So, early one morning, with a BaAka tracker and Dr. Carroll in the lead, we headed deep into the forest. For nearly 6 hours we walked, hiked, and sloshed through jungly growth and streams, looking for signs of gorillas.

LOWLAND GORILLA

Our guides warned us that if we should see a gorilla, we musn't look it in the eye. The gorilla would take that as a challenge—a sign of aggression—and would most likely charge us. Even though these great apes are basically gentle creatures, they are naturally nervous and afraid of things they aren't familiar with. They are curious as well, and Dr. Carroll described times when a gorilla approached him, staring inquisitively and sometimes clapping its hands.

A Nest to Take a Rest In

Our guide pointed out signs of gorillas such as tracks, discarded food, and—most importantly—nests. Lowland gorillas travel in groups of between 5 and 10 members. Each animal makes a new nest of branches and leaves each day to rest and sleep in. The group might travel 2 miles and make a nest. The next morning they leave, walk another 1 or 2 miles in search of food, and then make another nest. The number of nests found close together indicates how large the group traveling together is. Six nests mean there are 6 gorillas in the group. Trackers can tell how fresh the nest is by the excrement the gorilla leaves behind. From the hair in the nest, they can tell not only the age of the gorilla, but also whether it is male or female.

Big Foot

A gorilla footprint is one of the signs a tracker is on the lookout for. This footprint measured 8 inches wide.

Stay Put!

If a gorilla comes toward you, do not run away. Stay where you are and lower your head slowly. Even if the gorilla gets close to you, it's all right, it will not touch you. But if you run away, the gorilla will run after you. When it catches you, it will bite you everywhere.

"Dr. Carroll told of many times when one of the BaAka trackers would stop, point, and say, 'The gorilla is right there, can you see it? It's eating.' Dr. Carroll said he would look and look, straining to see, but all he saw were leaves."

There is a gorilla in this photograph. Can you spot it?

There are two types of gorillas: mountain and lowland. Mountain gorillas, which live in Congo and Rwanda, don't move far each day. They leave obvious trails of where they've been, so it's quite easy to track and find them. But the lowland gorillas that live in the rain forest are constantly on the move. They are especially difficult to track in the dry season, when they travel deeper into the forest to look for food like fruit, bark, and the tender roots and shoots of young plants.

Gorillas live in small family groups led by an adult male who is usually over 10 years old and is known as a "silverback" because of the gray or silver hairs on the lower part of its back. The silverback is in charge of building nests and defending the group against danger. When threatened, a male gorilla beats its chest with its hands, roars and barks, and sometimes charges.

The rest of the group might include several females, infants, juveniles, and young males known as "blackbacks."

Staying in Touch

The field of vision in the rain forest is often very limited, so vocal signals between animals are more important than visual ones. Both gorillas and chimpanzees have a wide range of sounds to keep in touch with members of their group.

Female gorillas usually give birth to one baby at a time. A young gorilla stays with its mother for about 3 years.

Unlike mountain gorillas, lowland gorillas spend a lot of time in the trees and are very difficult to spot, especially for people like us who aren't trained to "see" in the forest. We come from places where there are visual points of reference—vistas and a horizon. In the forest there is no horizon, and our eyes don't easily adjust to viewing things in dense, tangled growth.

Several times we heard the deep-chested *ooo-ooo* sounds of gorillas echoing through the forest. To keep in contact with each other over short distances, gorillas also make a kind of low buzzing sound. Our guide described it as resembling someone deeply clearing his or her throat. Gorillas make the sound when they're relaxed—it's a way for them to stay in touch with each other while traveling and foraging through the forest.

Other sounds, such as barking, are more aggressive and may serve as warnings. Trackers have learned to recognize individual gorillas by the sounds they make. One male, an old silverback with a scar on its face, had a distinctive, horsey bark. When the trackers heard that particular call, they knew that "Scarface" was in the area.

Chimpanzees in the Trees

The other great apes of Dzanga-Sangha are chimpanzees. Like gorillas, they are secretive animals, but we would occasionally spot them, climbing and swinging about the lower and middle canopy of the forest. Whether we saw them or not, we could almost always hear them chattering and calling to one another.

Chimpanzees are extroverted, sociable animals that travel in small bands made up of males and females with their young. These bands, however,

Clever Nut-Cracking Chimps

Sometimes chimpanzees carry a "hammer"—a piece of wood or a stone—with them as they search for nuts in the trees. Placing the nut in a small indentation of a root, the chimpanzee repeatedly strikes it with the hammer. This way the nut cracks open cleanly and isn't smashed to small pieces.

LOWLAND GORILLAS

Gorillas and chimpanzees are both tailless primates that belong to the family of great apes. Found only in Africa, gorillas and chimpanzees are close relatives of humans.

An adult male lowland gorilla can reach a height of about 5 feet and weigh as much as 300 pounds, while adult females weigh about 165 pounds. Lowland gorillas are smaller than their mountain cousins, whose adult males can weigh up to 600 pounds. A lowland gorilla's coat is short and sparse compared to the long and silky fur of a mountain gorilla. A gorilla in the wild lives to be about 30 years old.

Gorillas usually walk about on all four limbs, supporting part of their weight on the knuckles of their hands, but occasionally they stand erect.

Chimpanzees also knuckle-walk, and they are agile climbers and spend much of their time in the trees.

A full-grown chimpanzee standing erect measures about 5 feet. Males weigh between 90 and 200 pounds, females between 66 and 175 pounds. Females give birth for the first time when they are around 12 years old. They usually have a single baby, sometimes twins, every 3 to 4 years.

Young males leave their mother after 5 to 10 years to hunt with bands of males, but females often spend their whole lives near their mother and extended family.

CHIMPANZEE

Highly intelligent, chimpanzees use tools such as sticks and grass to obtain insects from a termite mound.

are usually part of larger community of 80 or so chimps. They communicate with one another by using a variety of facial expressions and sounds, including screaming, hooting, and grunting.

Chimps spend half their waking hours foraging for food and feeding on flowers, fruits, leaves, seeds, and insects. Among their favorite foods are termites, and these highly intelligent apes use tools, such as twigs and grass, to poke into termite mounds and fish out the insects. Although they rarely eat meat, chimpanzees sometimes hunt birds, bush pigs, small monkeys, and rodents.

Each night, chimps bend small branches and twigs high up in the trees to build individual leafy nests to sleep in.

Beware!

The assassin bug is brightly colored to warn others that it will produce a strong, bad-smelling odor when threatened. Assassin bugs feed on millipedes on the forest floor.

ASSASSIN BUG

Only about 200,000 chimps live in all of Africa, and they are considered an endangered species. It is illegal to hunt them, and in the Dzanga-Sangha Reserve they have been carefully and successfully protected. But in many other areas, chimps are captured for the pet trade or for medical research. Their fate, like that of gorillas and elephants, is entwined with the fate of the forest. These large animals need room to roam and hunt. When areas are cleared for farming or logging, part of their essential habitat is gone forever.

"One day we came upon a large group of chimpanzees in the trees. They began to make an incredible fuss, yelling, screaming, hooting, and clapping. Then they pooped in their hands and threw it down at us. They wanted us to go away. It worked."

A Lot like Us

Many local people have always refused to hunt chimpanzees because they bear so many similarities to human beings. They have very expressive faces and, like us, can be recognized by their individual facial features.

Life
at
the
Lodge

9

"I've named the enormous spider on my ceiling Herman. He hasn't moved in a week."

Every morning, those of us at Doli Lodge would meet on the veranda for breakfast. The corn-flakes were soggy and the sugar pops were covered with ants. No one ever ate the cereal, but it was always there. Instead, we drink the usual strong coffee, brush the flies off the bread, and have a serving of the heavily sweet-ened canned fruit and a slice of pineapple.

"Any food set out was immediately covered with ants and flies."

Lizards of all sizes would sit on tree branches as the sun came up and warmed the bark. Although we couldn't always see them, we heard monkeys and birds moving through the forest canopy.

After breakfast, we headed into the forest to begin another day of collecting, photographing, and filming. After 5 weeks, the heat, insects, and long, hard hours began to wear on us. Some of the work was fascinating, but some was boring and

Sing Along

Adding to the "music" of the forest, grasshoppers make chirping sounds by rubbing their scrapers together. Found on the inside of each back leg, scrapers have a comb-like row of ridges.

AFRICAN GRASSHOPPER

repetitive. In general we'd learned to live with the cockroaches and the continual dampness—nothing was ever quite dry, not sheets, towels, or clothes. Paper was always damp and absorbed the ink from our pens, the letters swelling up into fat, wormy lines on the page.

The collecting site was a 40-minute walk from the lodge. At the end of the day, we'd head back along a dirt road cut through the forest.

The sights, sounds, and smells of the rain forest surrounded us. Fallen leaves, fruit, and pods were underfoot. Overhead was the densely packed canopy of green, which gave us the feeling of being in constant twilight.

We would look up, knowing there were many thousands of animals that made their homes in the

Jump!

The 8 eyes of a jumping spider are arranged in 3 rows. The largest pair of eyes are on the top row and face forward. These spiders have the sharpest vision of all spiders. In addition to their excellent eyesight, they are able to make spectacular jumping leaps.

Keen eyesight, along with its ability to leap long distances, makes the jumping spider an extremely effective hunter.

Building a Pirogue

For centuries, the people of Dzanga-Sangha have used pirogues, or dugout canoes, to travel, fish, and trade along the Sangha River and its tributaries. These narrow wooden boats glide easily along the rivers and through swamps filled with low-lying palm trees and thick reeds where other crafts would have difficulty manuevering.

To build a pirogue, the boatmaker uses a large tree with a straight trunk. He shapes the trunk and hollows it out with a machete or ax. The traditional method of hollowing out the trunk is to burn it with hot coals. The boatmaker then uses a wooden tool shaped much like a shoehorn to smooth the inside curve of the pirogue.

trees, from butterflies and frogs to monkeys and chimpanzees. The diurnal animals—those that are active during the day—were getting ready to bed down for the night. The nocturnal animals—those that sleep during the day and hunt at night—were waking up.

We knew that plants have developed endless ways to make themselves noticed by the animals that eat and spread their seeds. In the crowded environment of the rain forest, where it is often impossible to see, animals have also devised many ways of communicating. The movements and noises we heard might be signals for any number of things. There are sounds to keep in touch with their

Go Fish

Fishing spiders divide their time between land and water. They scurry along the shoreline, foraging among plants and rocks for insects. They also pursue and capture prey in the water, remaining under the surface for as long as 30 minutes as they hunt water insects, minnows, and tadpoles.

FISHING SPIDER

young and sounds to find a mate. Certain noises are designed to frighten a predator or to warn others in their group that there is danger. Some are social "calls"—ways for animals to stay in touch with one another while hunting and foraging through the tangle of vines and branches. All around us, there was an intense feeling of life and movement. If only our senses were stronger and our knowledge deeper, what a marvel of information we would be able to obtain from just walking through the rain forest!

"Mystery Meat" and a River View

We met for dinner every evening and discussed the day's work. The food wasn't bad. We usually had plantains, potatoes, onion soup, or beans. Sometimes we had eggplant, rice, tough beef, or a stew made with what we began to call "mystery meat," which showed up in various forms for breakfast, lunch, and dinner.

> "The mystery meat shows up again and again. Whatever it is, it's been cooked to resemble some of the trees we've been collecting."

From the wide, open dining hall and veranda, we had a wonderful view of the river.

Hippopotamuses grazed on the shore. Flocks of fantastic-looking birds—giant kingfishers, palm-nut vultures, plovers, terns, and sandpipers—passed overhead. Some stopped to feed on the sandbars.

On several occasions, a group of children played on the sandbar. It looked as if they were practicing karate moves, and they put on quite a show for us.

Local boatsmen from Bayanga passed by in pirogues or small wooden boats. In the early

Social Insect

Social wasps live in large nests that look and feel like paper, but are actually made of plant matter. While most wasps leave after depositing food for their eggs, female social wasps take care of their young daily. They lay and tend to one egg at a time, feeding it caterpillars ground into paste.

Monsters and Spirits

Like people all over the world, the people of the forest have stories and legends that have been passed down from generation to generation. Some are about mythical beasts or monsters that haunt the forest or rivers. Here are a few of these stories.

In the black waters of the Sangha River lives a two-headed serpent named **Yohole**. After the sun sets, Yohole rises from the depths of the river and waits for any piroguers who have stayed out too late. When Yohole spots a boat, he entwines his two heads to block the river's flow. Whichever head is quicker gets the boatman; the other gets his catch of fish.

Hidden in the reeds is a monster with the body of a man and the head of a bird. His name is **Mondjole.** He feeds on fish, but if he hasn't caught enough, he will snap up the catch of a fisherman with his large beak.

There are some friendlier spirits that live along the river. **Boyobes**, small creatures covered with gray fur, often speak with the BaAka hunters in a language of squeaks, revealing the secret hideouts of the animals the hunters are seeking.

evening there was a steady stream of them travel-ing up and down the river on their way home. They greeted us, waving and calling, and we greeted them in return. Often they would sing and call back and forth to each other, their voices soaring in call and response.

Because of the way the rivers flow together, many different African societies—and linguistic and cultural groups—have come together in the Dzanga-Sangha region. Since groups of Bantu-speaking people migrated here hundreds of years ago, the rivers have served as highways and places of trade. There are few roads in this part of Africa, so people travel from village to village by pirogue or canoe.

The pirogue is the most common way to get around. The boatmen run a river taxi service, transporting people up and down the river to the

Haa-Haa-Haa

The hadada ibis is known for—and named for—the loud *haa-haa-haa-de-dah* call it sounds when flying to and from its roost.

NILE MONITOR LIZARD

The largest African lizard is the Nile, or water, monitor, a stout-bodied reptile with powerful limbs and strong claws. Common in river valleys, it is an excellent swimmer, using its long, oarlike tail to propel itself through the water. It can be seen basking on rocks or tree stumps. The teeth of adults are rounded and peg-shaped—ideal for crunching on crabs and mussels, for which they forage in freshwater pools. They also feed on frogs, fish, birds, and unattended crocodile eggs. Adult monitor lizards are a grayish brown color, but the young are beautifully patterned in vivid yellow and black.

The name *hippopotamus* means "river horse," even though this animal looks like a pig and is closely related to pigs. Full-grown hippopotamuses weigh more than 3 tons and measure up to 13 feet long. Their mouths, which can open 4 feet wide, contain long, white tusks and large teeth for crunching the grasses and reeds they feed on.

Hippopotamuses are more active at night, after spending most of the day lying in muddy water with only their nostrils and eyes above the surface. They are good swimmers and can stay under water for 10 minutes at a time with their eyes and ears tightly closed.

Don't Sweat It

A hippopotamus has an almost hairless, spongy hide, which in some places is often 2 inches thick. It is commonly thought that hippopotamuses sweat blood because their hides are frequently covered in a red-colored, shiny liquid. What really happens is that a thick, pinkish oil is released from their skin glands when the animals leave the water. The oil protects the skin from the drying effects of the air, and gives the hippo a glossy sheen.

The Sangha River is one of the three major tributaries, or smaller rivers, that feed the Congo River. Long before the first European explorers arrived in the 1890s, the Sangha River was a trade route for the shipping of slaves, ivory, fish, medicines, palm oil and wine, and rubber.

villages. They also carry goods to and from market-places. Piroguers trade for all kinds of things, even clothes, so they are sometimes seen wearing base-ball caps and jeans, which they've traded for on their route.

Travel by pirogue is hardly easy. The boaters must steer clear of crocodiles. What may look like a gray boulder in the water could be a hippopotamus. To safeguard against such dangers, piroguers tend to guide their boats close to shore.

Many piroguers are expert at fishing, casting nets from their boats or stringing net traps across the river. Sometimes they also use "cast nets," flat spheres that open up in the water. The weighted nets drop to the river bottom, and the catch is then pulled in by the fishermen.

Tapping for "Palm Wine"

Piroguers routinely supply villagers along the shore with "palm wine," which they make from the sap of *raphia* palm trees.

One day, we took a trip upriver with one of the piroguers. He guided us into a beautiful swampy area covered with waterlilies and reeds that made it look like a floating garden. We stopped at one of the

A rain forest flower.

AFRICAN SLENDER-SNOUTED CROCODILE

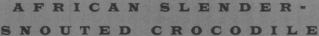

With its long, tapering jaw, the slender-snouted crocodile catches fish as it glides through the water. Able to stay underwater for up to an hour, this crocodile also hunts crabs, frogs, and snakes. Females nest along the riverbanks, laying from 13 to 27 eggs at a time. A slender-snouted crocodile never stops growing throughout its lifetime, which can be as long as 50 years. During that time, it will go through thousands of teeth, which are replaced as soon as one falls out or wears out.

points of high ground where the palm trees grew. He pulled the boat up alongside one of the trees, which have thick, squat trunks. Our guide cut a V-shaped notch into the top of the tree and, using a strip of old tire, strapped a plastic bottle around the trunk in order to catch the milky fluid. We each took a sip. When it's freshly tapped, it tastes slightly sweet and much like coconut milk. It takes several days of fermentation until it becomes "wine."

"For some unexplained reason, several of us have started talking like pirates. We are endlessly amused by our antics, but some of the others are ready to make us walk the plank—aaargh, matey! Call it jungle fever. Tonight we played cards and had more swashbuckling fun."

Many families who live along the river have their own palm tree, and everyone knows which belongs to whom. The sale of "palm wine" to people living in Bayanga or to tourists is a source of income for some families.

Good Night, Cockroaches

After dinner, we would spread the plans for the exhibit on the table. We discussed what we had accomplished during the day and made plans for the next day's work. Then some of us

A Crocodile's Dentist

The crocodile bird, or Egyptian plover, is a noisy shorebird that lays its eggs on sandbars along rivers. Before leaving the nest, the parent completely covers the eggs or chicks with sand to protect them from the heat. This plover is known as the crocodile bird because it will sit coolly in the huge, gaping mouth of a crocodile, picking leeches, flukes, and tsetse flies from the animal's teeth and gums. Apparently it cleans the crocodile's teeth in return for dinner. This type of relationship, in which animals benefit from each other, is called a symbiotic, or "mutualistic," relationship.

Basketball—
Bayanga-Style

"The people who worked at the lodge—the cooks, waiters, room cleaners, and guards—were happy to have their jobs. They were friendly, and we were on a first-name basis with many of them.

We began talking to them about playing basketball in Bayanga, and they challenged us to a game. Supposing that no one here had

played much, we thought it would be a small pickup game or perhaps just some casual shooting.

We couldn't have been more wrong.

We arrived in Bayanga to find that a full court had been chalked off. Massive local redwood posts supported perfect nets and rims. The local doctor, who is a basketball fan, had donated the court to the town. Plus he also played with the opposing team, all of whom were quite large and decked out in uniforms and very nice basketball shoes. There was no question—our side was getting nervous.

We warmed up as a crowd of villagers began to assemble, and then the game started. I played hard—harder and more seriously than I wanted to—but by now there was a large crowd watching. At least 400 villagers surrounded the court. Everyone was taking it seriously, and the competition was fierce. The temperature was over 100 degrees Fahrenheit. At half-time I was overheated and so exhausted I was afraid I'd pass out.

We told the other team (and anyone else who would listen) that we were scientists and artists, not athletes. We also said we weren't used to the climate, but I'm not sure we drew any sympathy. I guess they figured that since we were Americans, we'd all be able to play like Michael Jordan.

The final outcome, while not totally humiliating, was a decisive victory for their side. There were handshakes all around and we walked, exhausted but happy, back through the village."

A galago peers out
from its home inside
a tree.

played cards or went to our rooms to write letters home, made notes in our journals, or read.

Occasionally, several of us would take a nighttime walk through the forest. We put on our headlamps and headed out. The forest at night was cool, and a heavy mist hung in the air.

In the darkness, we felt as if we were walking down a tunnel, with blackness all around us. The narrow beam from our headlamps lit the way. In the moonlight, the looped and twisted vines looked like snakes hanging from the trees. Howls and screeches, whoops and chirps echoed through the night. We saw our breath in the mist.

> "I slept with a flashlight beside me so I could find my way to the bathroom in the middle of the night. I'd put on my flip-flops, turn on the flashlight, and check the floor for roaches. Then I'd crawl out and open the bathroom door—it squeaked really loudly—and say "hi" to the roaches in there."

In the night forest, we had no sense of north, south, east, or west. We kept to the elephant trails and depended on our sense of direction.

The beam of our lamps caught the eyes of an animal crouched in a tree. Reflecting the light, its eyes looked like glowing, amber coals—what is known as "eyeshine." For an instant our lights blinded the animal, and it froze. We thought it was a small owl, but it turned out to be a bushbaby, or galago. They can leap tremendous distances and quite suddenly, seemingly out of nowhere, appear on a branch.

Big-Eyed Bushbaby

The galago, sometimes called a bushbaby, is a small tree-dwelling primate. It spends its day curled up in the hollows of trees or in soft nests, sleeping. Galagos have gray or brown soft, woolly fur, large eyes, long hind legs, and long tails. They are able to fold back their large ears, apparently to protect them while leaping from tree branch to tree branch. A galago's neck is so flexible it can turn its head completely around to see behind itself.

TIGER MOTH

One evening we caught sight of a potto, also called a tree bear or a softly-softly. This small, slow-moving tree dweller is a primate that feeds on fruit, small animals, and insects. It is thought to be one of the best climbers in the forest, with an extraordi-narily strong grasp. The local people fear trying to catch it, afraid that it will grab them and it will be impossible to break them-selves free. In fact, the name "potto" comes from a word in an African dialect and means "the animal that holds tight."

"I was wondering if I could live here, but I would never be able to tolerate the heat, humidity, and lack of comforts like hot water. But this would be a pretty boring trip if everything was just like home."

The night walks were exciting, but it was always a relief to get back to the safety of the lodge and crawl into bed for the night.

Our beds were made of wooden frames with a thin mattress. The pillow was hard and lumpy, so most of us rolled up clothes and stuffed them into the pillow-case. Each bed was draped with mosquito netting—a necessity for preventing us from being eaten alive by insects in the night. We fell asleep to the sounds of scut-tling cockroaches and spiders in our rooms, and the deep, distant hum of the forest beyond.

Flying by Sound

Bats are among the many night hunters in the forest. They navigate through the forest not by sight, but by a method know as echoloca-tion. A bat emits high-pitched, pulsing sounds that bounce off objects and sur-faces in the bat's way. The echo comes back to the bat, which analyzes the sound to orient itself, to avoid fly-ing into obstacles, and to find food.

SHORT-HORNED GRASSHOPPER

Last Days

10

> **"Suddenly there was nothing to do, and I'm just too tired to do any more adventuring."**

The last week was chaotic. There was a lot of last-minute collecting of plants and packing to be done. Those of us on the film crew had recorded more than 46 hours of tapes, but there was still more to do. We had filmed segments on threats to the forest such as logging and farming. We also visited the remains of an old diamond mine—a series of square pits 6 to 8 feet deep dug into the sand. We filmed it to show how mining tears up the land and causes extensive damage. Sights like this illustrated what we wanted to show in the exhibit about the threats to the rain forest. But there was another aspect of the problem, and that was poaching—the illegal killing of animals for their meat, skins, or tusks.

> "Poaching is a big problem for the simple reason that people like to eat meat," one of the park wardens told us. "Also, it is an easy way to make money."

There were two kinds of poachers—local people, and people from outside the forest who kill animals for sport. Sometimes, local people hunt simply to feed themselves and their families, but many are poor and jobs are scarce, so some hunt animals in order to sell the meat. Poaching is a complicated problem, and there are no easy answers.

Hanging Out

The epaulet bat gets its name because of the tufts of white fur on its shoulders, which resemble epaulets, or shoulder decorations like those on a military uniform. Measuring about 5 1/2 inches, this bat eats clinging to a branch with one foot.

In the Dzanga-Sangha Reserve, park wardens patrol the forest to keep animals safe from illegal hunting. Creating and maintaining a protected area means conserving its natural resources. But it also means meeting the needs of people who depend on those natural resources.

Packing Up

Packing was difficult and time consuming. Each leaf and twig had to be individually wrapped in layers of waxed paper, then laid in boxes and crates. Woody shrubs and trees had to be sprayed with preservative to prevent mold. Grasses and leaf litter had to be placed in sealed crates.

"When I think of what is involved when we get back to New York and start putting the exhibit together, it seems quite overwhelming."

When we were finished, there were a total of 58 crates—over 10,000 pounds—to be sent by ship from Africa to the United States.

In our last days, we also spent time cleaning up Doli Lodge, the safari camp, and the forest itself. We removed all the plastic markers and tags we had put on the trees and vines. There was a chance the elephants might eat them, and the plastic would surely make them sick. Each mist net had to be carefully taken down and every scrap of leaf or twig removed from it.

A Colorful Character

The rhinoceros viper has large, hornlike scales on the end of its snout. This thick-bodied snake grows to about 4 feet and has a complicated pattern of blue, black, purple, red, and yellow running down its back.

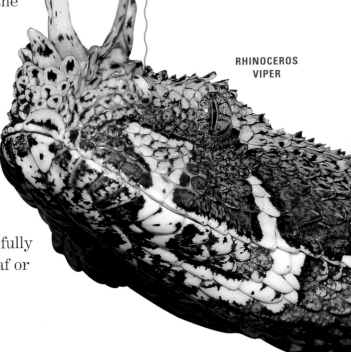

RHINOCEROS VIPER

Hunters

"On the last day we were there, while on the beach near the safari camp, I heard a strange noise, a kind of jingling sound. Walking along the river trail was a pack of small hunting dogs, followed by four BaAka hunters. Each dog had curious-looking, carved wooden "jingle bells" tied around its neck.

The men were, for the most part, naked, except for worn-out shorts. They were carrying long spears and bundles of nets over their shoulders.

The dogs continued along the trail, but the hunters stopped and crossed the beach to where I was working. The leader of the group offered his hand in friendship. As we shook hands he said something I didn't understand, but I had the feeling that he was welcoming me. I was struck by his and the other hunters' presence and poise. Although I'm sure they didn't understand a word I said, I told them how magnificent their country was and how beautiful their forest. Then they turned and walked across the beach, vanishing into the forest to join their dogs. They had hunting to do."

Before we left, some of us got a chance to go the Independence Day parade in Bayanga. The villagers had hung Central African Republic flags at each end of Bayanga's main road. The parade set out from the basketball court, and crowds lined the road to watch as drummers played. Led by the village mayor, the parade

> "Boy, have I got stories to tell."

included schoolchildren, groups carrying banners, and the basketball team. At the end of the parade were clowns who wore army helmets and padded clothing to give their bodies unusual shapes. Some of the village women dressed up for the occasion in beautifully printed fabrics and matching turbans.

SCARAB BEETLE

54 TONS AND 5 YEARS LATER . . .

We were not the first scientists from the American Museum of Natural History to go to an African rain forest on a collecting expedition. In 1909, Herbert Lang and James Chapin traveled to the Congo basin rain forest. Five years later, they returned with 100,000 insects, 10,000 photographs, and thousands of artifacts—over 54 tons of material which they shipped by boat to New York City. They calculated they had hired more than 38,000 local people to help move the crates through the forest.

Above: A hand-colored lantern slide of an African chief taken by Herbert Lang in 1913.

On our final night in Dzanga-Sangha, we held a farewell party at Doli Lodge. We presented Museum T-shirts and hats to the lodge workers, our guides, and other helpers. We thanked them and said our good-byes. That night we fell asleep to the sound of drums and singing in the distance. We wondered what they meant, and thought perhaps it had something to do with the fact that someone in Auguste's family had died. We had heard there would be ceremonies in his memory.

"I keep wondering about my priorities. How can I come to places like this more often? How can I contribute more to the world? I'd like to be able to help people improve their lives, and help our natural world last a little longer."

We were ready to leave at 7:00 the next morning. We listened carefully to all the early morning sounds we'd come to know so well—the forest waking up to another day, the birds in the distance, the songs of the piroguers.

As the small plane took off, we looked down to see the tin roofs of the village of Bayanga and beyond—to the great rolling green expanse of forest. Then the plane turned and headed north— toward home.

So Long!

There are not many earthworms in the rain forest, but those that do exist can reach monstrous proportions. One giant species measures over 3 feet in length.

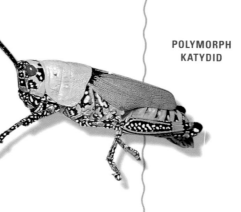

POLYMORPH KATYDID

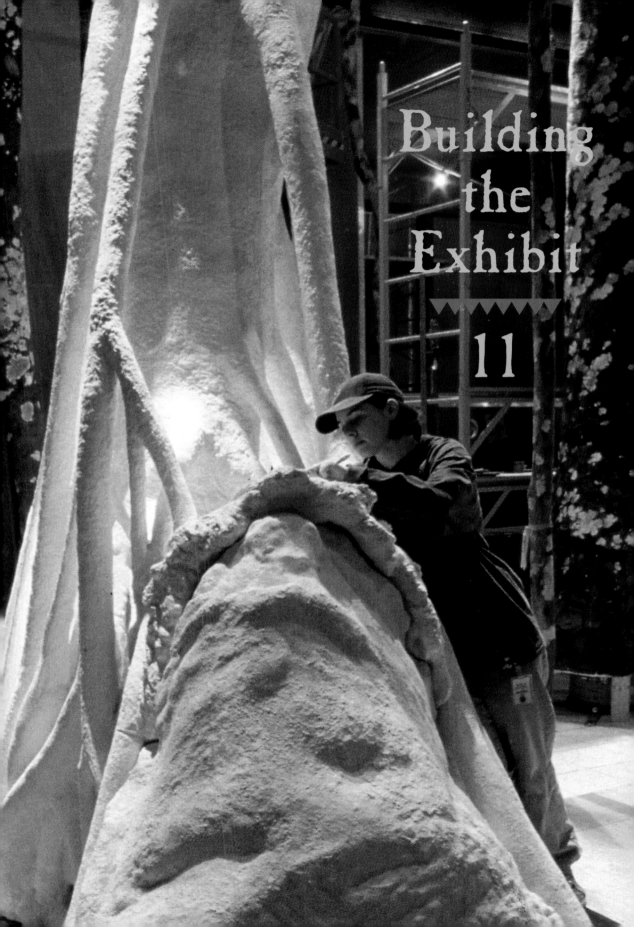

Building
the
Exhibit

▼▼▼▼▼

11

> **"We had to create a rain forest that not only looked real, but was also scientifically accurate."**

After 2 ½ months the containers of vines, tree trunks, and leaves we had so carefully packed in Africa arrived in New York. While waiting for the shipment, we constructed a small three-dimensional model of the rain forest diorama, so when the crates showed up, we were ready to get to work. Out came all the material we needed to begin building the forest—"leaf cookies" and rubber molds of tree bark, along with the real vines and leaf litter we'd collected from the forest floor.

For the trunks of trees we were going to build, we used huge cardboard tubes that carpets are usually rolled on. We wrapped them with rubberlike casts of bark created from impressions we'd made from the trees in Africa. Using photographs and sketches we'd made in the rain forest, we painted the tree trunks to look like the ones in Dzanga-Sangha. Tree branches were created from metal tubes wrapped in rubber and then painted.

In order to fill the branches of the trees we made, we would need 411,000 leaves! This is where the leaf cookies we'd made in Dzanga-Sangha came in. The cookies were imbedded in a plaster block. A machine, much like a big steam press, molded thin sheets of plastic over the plaster block, recording every detail of the leaves. When the whole process was finished, we had sheet upon sheet of leaves. For

How to Make a Rain Forest

A small-scale rain forest, complete with tiny trees and plants, would serve as a model for the life-size exhibit.

weeks workers cut leaves from the plastic sheets, painted them, and glued a wire to the base of each leaf to serve as a stem. Some leaves were even painted with fungus spots, and many were folded slightly or had holes made in them, as if insects had been nibbling on them. Finally the leaves were inserted, one by one, into holes drilled into the branches of the rain forest trees.

On the floor of the diorama we placed the dried leaves we'd brought back from Africa. To make them look as wet as they do in the rain forest, we coated them with a paste. For 18 months, we worked on building the diorama, and slowly it began to take shape. Trees towered over us. A stream ran along the forest floor. On tape we heard the sounds of the forest, and on the video-wall background, we glimpsed animals moving through the foliage.

At one time dioramas were a way visitors could see sights they had never seen—endangered animals and landscapes from faraway countries—that could be preserved only in a museum. The rain forest diorama is one of the first created with 21st century technology, yet many of the basic techniques, such as making and painting trees and leaves, are the same as those used over 100 years ago. The goal of the Museum remains the same also—to bring to visitors the beauty and purpose of the natural world in the hope that we will all be encouraged to understand, respect, and preserve it.

A rain forest tree trunk made from a huge cardboard tube wrapped with a rubberlike cast of bark.

Photography Credits